THE FISH BOOK

THE FISH BOOK

A SEAFOOD MENU COOKBOOK

By Kelly McCune

Designed by Thomas Ingalls
Photography by Victor Budnik
Food Styling by Sandra Cook

PERENNIAL LIBRARY

HARPER & ROW, PUBLISHERS, NEW YORK
Cambridge, Philadelphia, San Francisco, Washington
London, Mexico City, São Paulo, Singapore, Sydney

We dedicate this book to
Rob Miller and Susan Hopper
for their affection, their patience,
and above all for their palates.

For information address:
Harper & Row, Publishers, Inc.
10 East 53rd Street
New York, NY 10022
Published simultaneously in Canada by
Fitzhenry & Whiteside Limited, Toronto

Printed in Japan

FIRST EDITION

Quotation on page 5 from
The Compleat Angler by Izaak Walton.
Copyright 1985 by Penguin Books Ltd.
Reprinted by permission.

Book and Cover Design:
Thomas Ingalls + Associates
Photography and Set Design:
Victor Budnik
Food Styling and Props:
Sandra Cook
Assistants to Photographer:
Denise Cannon
Caroline Cory
Assistant to Stylist:
Helen Casartelli

**Library of Congress
Cataloging-in-Publication Data**

McCune, Kelly.
    The fish book.

    Bibliography: p.
    Includes index.
    1. Cookery (Fish)   2. Cookery (Shellfish)
3. Menus.
I. Ingalls, Thomas.   II. Title.
TX747.M227   1988   641.6'92   87-45639
ISBN 0-06-096201-1 (pbk.)

88 89 90 91 92 10 9 8 7 6 5 4 3 2 1

Acknowledgements

Thank you Gail Grant and Amanda
Bryan for your keen eyes and your
design support.

Thanks to Kevin McCurdy for the fine
fish from California Crayfish in San
Francisco, Dale Sims for the delicious
fish and shellfish from Gulfwater in San
Francisco, and to Dafine Engstrom and
John Wiest at Tsar Nicoulai of California
Sunshine Foods for their helpful infor-
mation about caviar.

Special thanks to Karen Hazarian for
the copper colander.

Thanks to Dianne McKenzie for her
attractive backgrounds.

Thanks to Mary Edwards for all the
wonderful plates and props she
graciously loaned.

Thanks to Peter di Grazia for loaning us
his fishing gear and to Doug Dufrene
for the use of his beautiful glass plates.

Our thanks to Sherry Phelan, Roberto
Varriale, Will Barker, Carrie Wong, and
Lori Nunokawa of Prime for the custom
surfaces and backgrounds. Thanks also
to J. Goldsmith Antiques for the interesting props, and to *Au Bain Marie,* Paris,
for their fine selection and helpfulness.

Thank you Bert, Jimmy, Laura, and
Nellie of Real Foods in San Francisco
for all the real help and superior
ingredients.

Thank you Carolyn Miller for editing
the manuscript and for your helpful
suggestions.

Thank you Deborah Stone for the
fine index.

Lastly, thank you Pat Brown for your
enthusiasm and inspiration.

But we'll take no care
When the weather proves fair
Nor will we vex now, though it rain;
We'll banish all sorrow
And sing till tomorrow,
And Angle and Angle again.

IZAAK WALTON
The Compleat Angler, 1653
from The Angler's Song

Contents

The earliest known fish hook was created over twenty-seven thousand years ago in France, the net came into existence by 8000 B.C., and the ancient Egyptians developed a healthy export business in dried salted fish that went on for centuries. The Romans ate fish on Fridays in honor of the goddess Venus, who was, according to legend, born of the sea on a halfshell. The early Christians, for whom the fish was an icon of their belief, incorporated this fish-eating ritual into their dietary laws as a symbol of Christ's fast.

For several centuries herring was as critical to international relations among European countries as oil is in the world market today, and many wars were fought over control of the most lucrative fishing regions. The early colonists were attracted to the New World primarily for its abundance of cod–that fish turned early American seaports into very profitable salt cod export communities. Boston still honors the "sacred cod" as the mascot of a town made wealthy by it. And Cape Cod was named for its connection with America's first big business. The Jamestown settlers were taught the clambake by the Indians, and even that town's down-and-outers had oysters to subsist on.

Although America's tradition of fish eating had an early start, it has, until recently, been on a steady decline. The Japanese, for example, eat nearly four times the amount of fish per person that we do. In recent years, however, our demand for fish has been rising. As we discover the many natural benefits of eating fish, more and more people are preparing it at home.

Fish is low in calories and low in fat. The fat or oil it does contain is either unsaturated or polyunsaturated, compared with the saturated animal fat found in beef. Polyunsaturated fish oil has been reported to help keep cholesterol, the primary contributor to heart disease, in check. And replacing saturated-fat meats with fish may even *lower* cholesterol. Fish is also very high in protein, so you don't have to eat more of it to get the protein you need. It has, in fact, an average of 25 percent more protein than beef.

New fish markets are opening all over the country in response to the growing interest in fish. Supermarkets that never carried it at all are adding a fish counter with properly displayed fresh fish, and a fishmonger behind it. Improved transportation brings ocean fish inland to midwestern markets within days, and refrigerated jet transport makes it possible for Americans to enjoy New Zealand clams, Dover sole, swordfish from Hawaii, and deep-water orange roughy. Freezing and icing techniques are improving, so freshness can be better maintained and depended upon.

The Fish Book presents new recipes and new ideas for preparing fish. We also draw on classic fish recipes, but adapt them to the developing taste for less fat and oil, and quicker, more straightforward preparation. Preparing fish does not have to be complicated. Fish cooks quickly, and the best way to keep it moist and tender is to *never overcook* it. The other important "secret" to delicious fish is freshness. And the higher quality fish we demand of our markets, the fresher it will be.

The Fish Book includes an extensive glossary of the freshwater and saltwater fish and shellfish available in this country, with a description of each fish, its common market names, the cuts available, and the cooking methods to which it is most suited. There are few standards for naming fish in the markets, so if the fish you are buying doesn't appear in the glossary, check the index. It may simply be listed under a different name.

Buying fish, cutting it up, and storing it are discussed in order to encourage you to experiment with different varieties of fish. Buy what is fresh that day and consult the glossary for methods of preparation, and the sauce chapter for a delicious complement. Avoid getting stuck on one or two familiar varieties–the different species have diverse flavors that combine with many different sauces and types of preparations. Some light is thrown on the question of what to serve with fish in Chapter 5, "Catch of the Day." Twenty-five complete menus, all with fish as the main course and sometimes as an appetizer or side dish, give suggestions and substitutions, and provide all sorts of possibilities for serving fish.

Fish is delicious, good for you, and quick to prepare. And in this fast-paced world, where we need to eat well to stay healthy but don't have lots of time, fish stands out as the perfect food.

CHAPTER 1

A Fish Glossary

A Fish Glossary

ABALONE
Other Names and Species: Ear shell, red abalone, sea ear

Saltwater/Pacific

The abalone is a univalve–a one-shelled mollusk–whose resemblance to the human ear has earned it its nicknames. Abalone is generally found along the Pacific coast, but overfishing has made it somewhat scarce. The harvesting of it is now regulated, and attempts are being made at controlled cultivation, which would make this delicious sea creature more widely available.

Abalone is usually found in steak form or live. Live abalone averages 4 pounds in weight and 6 inches in length. In either form it must be tenderized with a wooden mallet before cooking. Sauté steaks in butter less than a minute per side, or grill or broil them using high heat. Overcooking will toughen the meat.

ANCHOVY
Other Name and Species: Whitebait

Saltwater/Atlantic and Pacific

The anchovy is best known in its salt-cured form: oily fillets packed in neat rows in tins or pureed for paste. Anchovies are small fish with a high oil content, which lends them to the salt-cure treatment.

Anchovies are seldom marketed fresh, though when available they are usually served as "whitebait," small juvenile fish sprinkled with flour and quickly deep-fried.

Their flavor, cured or fresh, suggests herring or sardines, to both of which the anchovy is related. Cured anchovies may be rinsed to rid them of excess salt, if desired. To pan-dress fresh fish, twist off the head, pulling away the viscera with the head.

ANGLER
Other Names and Species: Allmouth, bellyfish, goosefish, monkfish, sea devil

Saltwater/Atlantic

Angler is most commonly found in the waters off the New England coast, where it feeds on crustaceans such as lobster and crab. Its average size is 12 pounds, though most of that weight is head. Only the tail of the angler contains meat.

The angler is so-named for the long flexible spine that extends from its dorsal fin, with which it "angles" for its dinner. The spine has a luminescent lure on the end that the angler waves in front of its mouth as bait. It lunges forward and snaps its huge jaw shut on even the crunchiest shellfish that might happen to get interested. Its fancy for sweet crustaceans–Cape Cod fishermen have a hard time keeping it out of their lobster traps–gives the angler a unique, lobsterlike flavor and texture that is excellent.

Angler is generally sold in fillet form, from which the skin must be removed. It is low in fat but does not dry out easily. Its firm, compact flesh adapts well to any cooking method from poaching to grilling, and its succulent flavor combines well with many sauces.

BASS
Saltwater Bass
Other Names and Species: Blackfish, black sea bass, Chilean sea bass, giant sea bass, grouper, hind, jewfish, Nassau grouper, rock bass, striped bass, striper, Warsaw grouper, white sea bass

Saltwater/Atlantic and Pacific

The bass family includes a large group of very diverse fish. They all come under the bass umbrella because of one common characteristic, and that is their very sharp, pointed dorsal fin. The name comes from the Old English word *byrst*, meaning "to bristle," which eventually became *barse*, the forerunner of our modern word. All bass have a similar mild flavor and their tender flesh separates into large flakes.

Black Sea Bass: Also *blackfish.* The Atlantic-dwelling black sea bass is one of the best of the saltwater sea basses. It is lean but not too dry when cooked, and has a delicate flavor due to its steady diet of crustaceans. Its firm texture lends itself to almost any cooking method. It is usually sold in whole, steak, or fillet form.

Giant Sea Bass: Sometimes marketed as *jewfish* or *grouper*, this Pacific Ocean bass has a rather bland flavor, but its white meat is quite lean. Recommended for stews and soups.

Grouper: Also *hind, jewfish, Nassau grouper, sea bass, Warsaw grouper.* There are a number of groupers, from both the Atlantic and Pacific coasts. Groupers are lean and firm with good flavor, and adapt well to many cooking methods, particularly those using moist heat. They are generally sold in steaks or fillets, which are virtually boneless.

Striped Bass: Also *rock bass, striper.* The striped bass runs in both salt water and fresh water, where it spawns (though there are some landlocked varieties, which are not as flavorful). It has a sweet flavor when quite fresh, and is suited to most cooking methods. The flavor declines rapidly after landing, however, so make sure yours is shiny silver and very fresh-looking. Striped bass fishing is temporarily controlled in some parts of the country, but the population is building and it should become one of the more widely available basses.

White Sea Bass: Also *Chilean sea bass, sea bass.* White sea bass is generally called simply sea bass in California, with the name of where it was caught sometimes attached. It has a finer texture than some basses, and a good flavor, though it tends to be dry if overcooked. Use a moist-heat cooking method, or baste or marinate it for broiling or grilling.

Freshwater Bass

Other Names and Species: Black bass, lake bass, striped bass, white bass, yellow bass

Freshwater

The freshwater basses are as ubiquitous as the saltwater varieties. There are dozens of species in American lakes, caught yearly by sportfishermen. Like the saltwater basses, their flavor is mild but pleasant, and the meat is lean.

Black Bass: Also *blackfish, black trout, Chinese bass, largemouth bass, Kentucky bass, lake bass, smallmouth bass, spotted bass.* The black bass and its many cousins are available in nearly every state in the Union. It has a delicate texture with fine bones, and is best when pan-fried in butter and oil the same day it is caught. Select the smaller ones (2 to 4 pounds) for eating. They have a better texture and flavor. The western U.S. black bass is popular in Chinese cuisine, and is usually marketed as blackfish.

Striped Bass: The landlocked variety of the striped bass (see above under Saltwater Bass).

White Bass: The freshwater white bass is nearly as common as the black bass. Its distinguishing marks are the long, narrow stripes down its sides, which show its relation to the striped bass. The white bass is lean and mild, and is best pan-fried.

BLACKFISH (1)

Other Names and Species: Tautog, wrasse

Saltwater/Atlantic

The blackfish is dark-gray, with puffy lips. It is generally caught under 3 pounds, and its firm, white, somewhat bland meat is best suited for soups and chowders.

BLACKFISH (2)

Another name for both black sea bass and black bass (see under Bass).

BLUEFISH

Other Names and Species: Chopper, fatback, snapper

Saltwater/Atlantic

Bluefish are well known to East Coast fishermen as "choppers," the marauding band of voracious eaters that leave behind a trail of fish bones and blood after their frenetic feedings. The name comes from the sound their teeth make when clicking together. Even the young ones are called "snappers." But fishermen also like the bluefish because it is a fighter, which makes for exciting sport.

The bluefish ranges in size from 4 to 8 pounds. It is an oily, dark-fleshed, soft fish that has a mild flavor. It is commonly found in fillet form, and these may have a dark muscle strip, which should be removed as it tends to be too oily and strongly flavored. Use a dry-heat cooking method such as grilling or broiling for bluefish. When grilling, leave the skin on so the fillet will hold together. Serve skin side down, but do not eat the skin (it's tough). Thin bluefish fillets do not need to be turned. Because of its oiliness, bluefish needs no baste or marinade, but is best with slightly acidic sauces, such as lemon, lime, tomato, or mustard.

BUTTERFISH

Other Names and Species: Harvestfish, Pacific pompano, pomfret

Saltwater/Atlantic

The butterfish gets its name from an easily deducible source: it has a very high fat content. It is found on the East Coast, though on the West Coast there is a similar fish called the sablefish (see under Sablefish). Butterfish has a mild, pleasant flavor, and a very delicate texture. Its gray flesh turns white when cooked.

The butterfish is generally found dressed, pan-dressed, or butterflied. Because of its high fat content, it is best pan-fried or broiled. When broiling, leave the skin intact and cook without turning.

CARP

Other Names and Species: Common carp, grass carp, silver carp

Freshwater

The carp has an interesting and long history as a food fish. It was one of the first cultivated fish in history, dating back to 500 B.C. in China. It was farmed in Europe as early as the eleventh century, and was introduced to America by the mid-1800s. In China and Japan, carp live in the bottoms of rice paddies and snack on leftovers from the kitchen. They have beautiful skin with mottled gold, orange, red, and brown spots, and are often used in ornamental ponds in Asian gardens. They are known to come when you clap, and are considered valuable for both dinner and decor.

The flaky white meat of the carp is mild and pleasant tasting. It is usually available as whole fish, steaks, or fillets, and is suited to most cooking methods. The dark strip of meat may be a bit tough, but it is richer tasting than the white meat and doesn't need to be cut away. Carp is the most commonly used fish in *gefilte fish*.

CATFISH

Other Names and Species: Blue catfish, channel catfish, mud catfish, white catfish

Freshwater/Mostly Southern U.S.

Catfish is a distinctly American fish and more precisely, a very *Southern* fish. The state of Mississippi leads the country in commercial catfish production with about 85 percent of the total. But catfish is currently gaining popularity in other parts of the country as well, with the opening of restaurants that specialize in Cajun, Creole, and Southern food. Commercially farmed catfish tend to be superior to the wild ones since they are fed a controlled diet and live in clear waters, and their availability will make catfish an increasingly popular choice.

The catfish is often sold as frozen fillets, which doesn't seem to harm its flavor if frozen properly. When fresh, it is usually marketed dressed, pan-dressed, or in fillet form. Have the fishmonger remove the sharp spines from the fins if you are purchasing the fish whole. Make sure the tough skin of the fish has been removed before cooking.

Catfish is most commonly prepared Southern style: deep-fried in a cornmeal batter with hush puppies (fried drops of batter) on the side. Catfish has a delightful freshwater flavor and moist, firm white meat that can be grilled, broiled, or poached, and that combines well with a number of sauces.

CASPIAN CAVIAR
(l. to r.): *Sevruga, Osetra, Beluga*

CHINESE CAVIAR
(l. to r.): *Mandarin Imperial, Beluga, Osetra*

Fresh whole carp

CAVIAR

Most of the world's true caviar comes to us from the Caspian Sea, where it was created over seven hundred years ago. It is now produced in the U.S.S.R. and Iran, which border the Caspian Sea, though a significant amount of it has recently come out of China's Amur River. Small quantities of it are also produced in the United States, Japan, and Europe. Unfortunately, both scarcity and politics have made caviar astronomically expensive and hard to get.

The word caviar comes from the Turkish word *havyar*, or "fish egg." It is traditionally considered to be the roe from the sturgeon, of which there are a number of species of varying size and quality. All caviar should be firm and moist. It should glisten, and have a rich look. Caviar must not look dimpled or dried-out. Good caviar is never tough or rubbery. You should be able to crush it on the roof of your mouth with your tongue. The finest caviar is deep golden in color, but this caviar is quite rare.

Most true caviar available today is light-gray to charcoal-gray. The lighter gray the caviar, the more expensive. Beluga caviar, the "top" caviar, is graded for both color and size: 000 is the finest and largest, 00 is next, and 0 is the smallest and darkest gray. Sevruga and osetra caviar are graded 1 for the highest quality and 2 for the next highest. Select only caviar marked *malossol*, which indicates that it has been cured with a minimum of salt–less than 4 percent.

Caviar is packed in tins sealed with a wide rubber band (this allows the oil to ooze out), or small jars with a pop-top like a bottle cap or a screw-top. Caviar will last for up to 12 months if stored in its original 4 pound tin at a constant temperature of 26 to 28 degrees Fahrenheit. However, household refrigerators stay at about 38 to 40 degrees, which will hold caviar for only 10 days. Ideally, store caviar tins well-wrapped in plastic in a bowl of ice in the refrigerator until ready to use. If carefully monitored, caviar will keep this way for 4 to 6 weeks. To store opened caviar, place a sheet of plastic wrap directly on top of the caviar, replace the top, and keep it no more than 1 week.

There are also a number of roes that are commonly called "caviar" but which are not from the sturgeon. These roes range in color from black to bright red. Since 1966, FDA regulations prevent the marketing of fish roe other than sturgeon as "caviar," so if you are buying a non-sturgeon caviar the package must indicate what fish it is from. Some of these caviars are dyed, supposedly to make them more marketable. This does not affect the flavor, but may leave a tinge of color in your mouth.

A jar of caviar that has been vacuum-sealed generally contains processed caviar. This caviar has been pasteurized, a process which flash cooks the roe at a temperature up to 160°. Processing does diminish the flavor, and makes the caviar rubbery.

Lesser-quality and substitute caviars can be served with condiments such as chopped onion or egg, lemon, or chives. Serve good caviar all by itself on ice with thin slices of lightly buttered bread or toast (and wash it down with some excellent freezer-cold vodka).

Golden or Imperial: This golden-colored caviar is considered to be the most exquisite caviar. The Caspian sterlet at one time yielded golden caviar, but it has mostly been fished out, making its caviar quite rare. Some golden caviar is still found in the Mandarin beluga sturgeon from the Amur River in China.

Beluga: Beluga caviar has become quite scarce in recent years, thus making it quite expensive. Its large pale-gray eggs come from the large "white" sturgeon which can weigh up to 2,000 pounds. These sturgeon are found in the Caspian Sea.

Mandarin Beluga: This newcomer to the market is also from a breed of the large "white" sturgeon. It can weigh up to 2,200 pounds, and is found in the Amur River of Northern China. The caviar has a jade-gray tinge.

Osetra (also *Osietr*): Osetra is Russian for sturgeon. This darker gray caviar is slighly smaller than beluga. It has a slightly nutty flavor, and is stronger than the beluga.

Mandarin Osetra: This Chinese caviar is slightly more assertive than its Caspian Sea counterpart. It is brownish-gray in color.

Sevruga: The sevruga is the smallest sturgeon used for caviar. The eggs are charcoal-gray, and are the smallest of the true caviars. They have an assertive, almost meaty flavor.

Pausnaya: This is not a type of caviar but rather descriptive of a type of preparation. *Pausnaya* caviar is made from roe that has been crushed or broken during the curing process, and is sold as a thick caviar spread.

Other Caviar

Whitefish: Also *golden, American golden.* Whitefish roe is naturally golden in color. It always comes frozen if it is fresh; otherwise it is pasteurized and sold in jars. Freezing whitefish roe does not damage its flavor or texture, though most other roes cannot withstand the extreme temperature. Thaw fresh-frozen roe in the refrigerator.

Lumpfish: Lumpfish roe is very often used as a caviar substitute. It is usually colored blackish-green or red, but will be labeled "lumpfish" caviar. This caviar is pasteurized and is rather salty, but it is quite good. If it is too salty it can be lightly rinsed in a fine-mesh strainer. Lumpfish caviar can be further improved with the condiments such as chopped egg, chopped onion, chives, or lemon.

Paddlefish: A very common caviar substitute, the paddlefish comes from the Mississippi River drainage system. The roe is greenish-black.

Salmon: The large bright red roe of the salmon is rapidly gaining popularity, particularly on the West Coast, where salmon are plentiful. The flavor is excellent and it is quite stunning to look at. The large red eggs can also be frozen, and are often sold frozen if fresh. Salmon roe is also pasteurized and sold in jars.

Flying Fish: This small orange roe is popular in Japanese cuisine, where it is called *tobiko.* It is sold either fresh or fresh-frozen.

Smelt: Another caviar used mostly in Japanese cuisine is *masago,* from the capelin. The roe is even tinier than the flying fish, and also bright orange.

Herring: Herring roe is also found in Japanese *sushi. Kazunoko* is generally marinated in a soy sauce mixture, which turns the roe clusters a yellow-gold.

Trout: This pale-yellow roe is not widely available, but attempts are being made to market it. It has a slightly earthy flavor.

Snail: Also *brut d'escargots, petit gris.* This "new" caviar has made an appearance in France. Its opaque, round eggs have a flavor more herb-like than fish-like, since the snails are fed fennel, rosemary, and thyme.

CLAM

Other Names and Species: Butter, cherrystone, chowder, geoduck, hardshell, horse, horseneck, littleneck, Manila, Pacific littleneck, pipi, Pismo, quahog, razor, rock, steamer

Saltwater/Atlantic and Pacific

Clams can be divided into two large categories: the hard-shell variety, and the soft-shell variety. Hard-shell clams do, in fact, have hard shells, but softshell clams don't have soft shells. Their shells are brittle and break easily, though, and the shells are not tightly closed. The neck of the soft-shell clam often protrudes from its shell.

Clams should be collected only during certain times of the year, and should be purchased from a reputable fishmonger, as they are subject to seasonal "red tide" (see page 43).

Hard-Shell Clams

Manila: These very small clams are from the Pacific Coast. They are quite tiny and can be eaten raw, or shucked for chowder (but that requires quite a few!).

Littleneck: The littleneck clam is another small hard-shell, and is delicious steamed, used in chowder, or eaten raw on the half shell. The name "littleneck" comes not from an anatomical description of the clam, but from the location of its heaviest population: Littleneck Bay, Long Island.

Pacific Littleneck: This clam variety is not related to its East Coast namesake, but is close in size. It is not well suited to eating raw, but is best steamed or used in chowder.

Cherrystone: Cherrystones are larger hard-shells than littlenecks, and can be eaten raw, steamed, or in chowder.

Quahog (pronounced co' hog): Also *chowder clam.* This is the next largest and therefore one of the toughest of the hard-shell clams. It is best suited to chowders or fritters.

Surf: The largest hard-shell, this clam is best sliced, pounded with a wooden mallet to tenderize, and batter-fried.

Soft-Shell Clams

Steamers: This common soft-shell is named for its most popular method of preparation. After steaming the clams open, first dip the meat in the strained cooking broth to swish off any residual sand, and then into melted butter on the way to your mouth. It's a classic treat. Steamers are mostly found on the East Coast, but some varieties exist on the West Coast as well.

Razor: Razor clams are almost never seen in the market because of the difficulty in collecting them without breaking their brittle shell. The shell resembles an old-fashioned straight razor, and is also just about as sharp as a straight razor along the edge. The elusive razor clam is able to dig itself straight down into the sand when threatened, thus making them very difficult to harvest.

Geoduck (pronounced *gooey duck*): This giant in the clam family is harvested from the Pacific. It has a long protruding siphon and is commonly seen in Chinese and Japanese markets. It is quite popular as *sushi*, and can also be sliced and tenderized for sautéing or used in chowder. To remove the black skin, dip the shucked clam into very hot water for 1 minute. The skin should peel off easily.

To Select Fresh Clams: Clams must be alive when cooked. They will feel slightly heavy, and have unbroken shells. Hard-shell clams should be closed or should snap shut when the muscle is pricked with the tip of a knife. The siphon, or neck, of a soft-shell will constrict when touched. Shucked clams packed in jars should be plump, with clear liquor containing no bits of broken shell.

To Clean and Soak Clams: Clams must be soaked in salted water to rid them of their sand. Scrub shells with a vegetable brush or clean them by agitating the clams in a sink filled with water so the shells rub together. Soak clams in a solution of 1/3 cup of salt in 1 gallon of water for 1 hour.

To Shuck Clams: Work over a bowl to collect the juices. Using a clam knife or a dull paring knife, work the blade in between the edges of the two shells until you can twist and pry upward. Do not cut the clam in half. Sever the top connector muscle and break off the top shell. Sever the bottom connector muscle to use the meat in your recipe, or spoon a little of the juice back in the shell and serve the clam raw on the half shell.

COD
Other Names and Species: Atlantic cod, cusk, haddock, hake, merluzzo, Pacific cod, pollock, salt cod, whiting

Saltwater/Atlantic and Pacific

The noble cod has a long history as a food fish. Before there was ice to transport fresh fish, cod was preserved by salt-curing and was eaten all through the winter. Cod was a major economic incentive to early colonists, who saw its abundance in the Atlantic waters off America as a pot of gold. Salted cod remains a very popular dish in most countries of Europe, more so than fresh.

Cod is a large family of related fish, of which there are over twenty types. The four major cod groups are cod, haddock, hake, and pollock, and these include many favorite varieties. The cod is a lean white fish with large flakes. It has a mild, pleasant flavor and does well cooked any way.

Atlantic Cod: This is the most common cod in existence. It is usually sold whole, pan-dressed, or as fillets. It is the fish that is often marketed as fish sticks, and it is also frequently salted.

Pacific Cod: The Pacific cod comes from the very northern part of the Pacific, above Oregon. It is very similar to Atlantic cod. It is not particularly abundant, and is often marketed frozen.

Cusk: This eastern fish is very abundant, but little marketed. Treat it like Atlantic and Pacific cod.

Scrod: Scrod is small cod.

Tomcod: This small fish is most often taken by amateur fishermen, since it is rarely over 10 inches.

Salt Cod: Salt-cured cod is delicious, and *not* salty. Look for white flesh, with the dark skin intact. Soak pieces in several changes of water for 12 hours, and whole salted cod for 24 hours. Poach the soaked fish for 15 minutes, or until it flakes. It may then be served with sauces, baked, sautéed, or used in stews or soups.

Haddock: Haddock has a finer texture than cod, and a slightly more refined flavor. It is smaller, from 2 to 5 pounds, but is most often sold as fillets. Finnan haddie is split smoked haddock, a tradition that began in Scotland where it is most likely to be found. Finnan haddie should be golden and moist, with a pleasing oak smoke aroma. Poach it before serving.

Hake: Also *silver hake, spotted hake, merlan, whiting*. There are a number of hakes, and they are quite abundant. They are less flavorful than cod or haddock, but are suited to most cooking methods.

Pollock: Also *Alaska pollock, Boston bluefish, coalfish, green cod, walleye pollock*. The pollock has darker flesh than the cod, but is very similar in texture. Its flavor is slightly bland, however. The Alaska or walleye pollock is gaining popularity. It is very small and has mainly been used for the imitation crab called *surimi*, but the flash-frozen fish is beginning to have a following.

CONCH
Other Names and Species: Edible pink, queen conch

Saltwater/Atlantic

The conch, pronounced "konk," is an edible marine snail like the abalone, whelk, and periwinkle. It comes mostly from the Florida Keys and farther south in warmer waters. The conch shell is a beautiful spiral-shaped knobby shell with a pointed end. The inside lip of the shell is a shiny pink or opalescent color.

The conch has a distinct and delightful flavor that anyone who has travelled to Jamaica or the Bahamas will remember from stews and fritters. To remove the conch muscle from the shell, drop the shell into boiling water and gently boil it for 10 minutes. Remove the shell and, holding it with a mitt, loosen the meat from the inside with a screwdriver (the tool that works best) and pull it down and away from the shell. Cut away the tentacles and dark parts. Conch meat must be sliced thinly and pounded with a wooden mallet to tenderize it.

Live blue crabs

CRAB

Other Names and Species: Alaska king, blue, Dungeness, Jonah, king, land, red, softshell, spider, stone.

Saltwater and Limited Freshwater/Atlantic and Pacific

Crab is one the most popular shellfish in this country, and it is fortunate that North America has more varieties of it than any other continent. The best way to eat crab is to buy it live and boil it, grill it, or steam it. Served with lots of melted butter, it's an unparalleled treat.

Blue Crab: The blue crab is *the* crab of the East Coast, particularly around Chesapeake Bay in Maryland. It has a blue oval shell with "wings" off each side, and a cream-colored underside highlighted with scarlet. The hardshell blue crab averages ½ pound.

Soft-Shell: The soft-shell crab is the blue crab in the stage between shedding its shell and growing a new one, a process the crab repeats dozens of times throughout its life

as it grows larger. The crabs are in this in-between state for only one week, so they are tricky to harvest. Generally, crabs that are just about to shed, called "busters," are held in boxes and hand-picked the moment they pop. The reason for the vigilance is that the other crabs would eat the soft, exposed creature in a moment. To prepare soft-shell crabs: Pull off the triangular apron on the crab's underside. Lift up the side flaps and pull off the spongy fingerlike gills. Cut off the face just behind the eyes. Dust the crab lightly with flour and sauté 3 to 5 minutes per side, or brush with butter and grill. Try grinding hazelnuts on the crabs while they're cooking.

Dungeness: The Dungeness is *the* crab of the West Coast, though it is currently in danger of being overfished. Dungeness crabs are larger than blues, ranging from 1½ to 4 pounds. They have a reddish shell and are available live, cooked whole, or as lump meat. Dungeness crab has a delicious sweet flavor.

King Crab: Also *Alaska king crab, Japanese crab.* These giant crabs come from the northern Pacific. They average 10 pounds, and are most commonly marketed as frozen cooked legs, since transporting them live would be impractical.

Stone Crab: Stone crabs are mostly harvested for their large claws. In fact, it is possible to harvest the claw without killing the crab, with the added bonus that the crab then will proceed to grow a new one (or "retread," as it is called in the business). Stone crab claws are distinctly tipped with black, and are generally marketed frozen. Their flavor is excellent, but unfortunately they are in short supply so the price may be high.

Land Crab, Red Crab, Spider or Snow Crab, Jonah: These crabs are not common but have tender, flavorful meat: the best are the land, Jonah, and red crabs.

To Kill a Live Crab: The best and most humane method is to drop the crab into boiling water for 1 minute, and then run it under cool water to stop the cooking. The crab will be killed the moment it hits the water. The crab is then ready to be cooked.

To Boil Live Crab: Drop the crab into boiling water and cook 10 to 12 minutes, until the shell is bright red.

To Remove Meat from Cooked Crab: Holding the crab by its legs, twist off the large top shell. The shell can be reserved for presentation or discarded. Lift up the breastplate (the triangular piece on the underside) and pull it off. From the top side, pull off the fingerlike gills on both sides of the body (these are often called the "dead man's fingers"). Remove the solid thin white tube (the intestine) and the grayish matter from the body. The yellow soft matter is the crab "butter" and is quite delicious blended into butter or sauces. Rinse the body. Only meat and shell should remain. Twist each leg off the body, and gently crack the shells with a mallet without bruising the meat.

CRAYFISH

Other Names and Species: Crawdad, crawfish, ecrevisse

Freshwater

Most crayfish come from Louisiana, but the Pacific Northwest is boasting a large harvest of late. These small crustaceans are related to and taste like the lobster, which certainly boosts their popularity. Most are about 5 inches long when marketed, and are sold live, cooked whole, or cooked and frozen. They are mostly tail meat, but the claw contains a bit of meat, and in the head is a tiny bit of orange "butter" that is also quite tasty.

Rinse the live crayfish well under running water or soak them in a sink filled with water for 15 minutes. Discard any dead crayfish. Drop live crayfish into boiling water, reduce the heat, and simmer for 7 minutes. To eat, use your fingers (it's easier). Twist off the tail, remove the tail shell, dip in butter, and eat.

DOLPHINFISH

Other Names and Species: Dorado, mahi-mahi

Saltwater/Atlantic and Pacific

This fish is not the mammal of the same name, nor does it look like it. But it has been so confused with the mammal that it is more commonly marketed under its Hawaiian name, *mahi-mahi*. The Hawaiians called it mahi-mahi, or "strong-strong," because it tends to fight the line. Dolphinfish occurs in warm oceans, and generally comes to us from Hawaii, or even more likely, from farther west.

The dolphinfish has firm white meat and a sweet flavor. It is marketed as steaks or fillets. It has a medium fat content and won't dry out when grilled or broiled. The skin should be removed before cooking.

Green-lipped mussels from New Zealand, and fresh scallops

DRUM

Other Names and Species: Atlantic croaker, corbina, croaker, redfish, spot, spotted seatrout, squeateague, totuava, weakfish, white sea bass

Saltwater/Atlantic and Pacific

The drum family is a large one that sometimes goes under the name of the croaker family. Its members are united by the fact that they all make a strange noise. Croakers sound more froglike, while drums make a noise more like drumming. But it all comes from the action of the gas bladder in this fish, which it contracts to make a distinctly audible sound. All drums have firm, lean white meat with a fine texture.

The Atlantic croaker is the most common family member, and is often sold simply pan-dressed. The corbina is more commonly known as a sport fish, but is tasty eating. The red drum is the redfish of blackened redfish fame, though it is now at risk of being over-harvested. The totuava comes from the Pacific, but is rarely seen. The white sea bass is well-known and quite abundant on the West Coast. The weakfish (so-called because its fragile mouth is easily torn by hooks) is quite flavorful, particularly pan-fried.

EEL

Other Names and Species: American eel, common eel, conger eel, silver eel

Saltwater and Freshwater/Atlantic

The eel is among the strangest of the world's fish, and there was until this century quite a cloud of mystery surrounding it. It was not known how the eel reproduced, or *where.* Aristotle thought eels came from the mud; early British ich-thyologists argued that eels simply evolved from seaweed. And these are only two of the wild specula-tions that have been made about eels over time. What actually happens is that the mature eel swims thousands of miles from the coastline, its usual habitat, out into the deep, deep ocean, to lay its eggs. Those eels then die, and are replaced by tiny invisible baby eels, which instinctively swim toward land. They gain color as they swim, finally arriving at their destination one to three years later! They live in the freshwater

estuaries and the shallow waters of American and European coastlines for up to ten years, after which time they head back out to sea to spawn and die.

Eels are not terribly popular in the United States, but in Japan the eel is supposed to bring good health if eaten during the summer solstice. Unagi (freshwater eel) and anago (marine eel) are also quite popular in the sushi bars.

Eels must be skinned before cooking. Have the fishmonger kill, dress, and skin the eel before you bring it home. Eels are best cut into 4-inch sections and poached, sautéed, fried, broiled, or stewed. Spaghetti-thin baby eels sautéed in butter and garlic are also a delicious treat.

FLOUNDER

Other Names and Species: Brill, fluke, plaice, sand dab, turbot, winter flounder, witch flounder, yellowtail flounder

Saltwater/Atlantic and Pacific

Flounder is one group in the large flatfish family, which also includes sole and halibut. Flounders are bottom dwellers, and have evolved with both eyes on their top side to watch for the enemy. They burrow when alarmed, and their dull brownish-gray coloring makes them hard to spot in the sand. What we call sole from our waters are really flounders, though they are closely related to the species of sole found in Europe. Flounders have firm white meat, a delicious flavor, and a fine texture. They are extremely easy to bone, especially after they are cooked: the entire skeleton can be lifted out once the top fillet is removed.

Winter Flounder: Also *lemon sole.* This is the most common American flounder. It is from the Atlantic, and averages 2 pounds. Winter flounder is usually sold simply as "flounder," in whole, pan-dressed, or fillet form.

Plaice and Sand Dab: These two closely related fish are small (usually under 1 pound), which makes them popular pan-fried or broiled fish. They are quite deli-cious, remain very moist, and have a sweet flavor.

Turbot: In this country, a turbot is a Pacific flatfish of no great distinction. In Europe, however, the species called turbot is a

diamond-shaped fish with great flavor, prized in French cuisine.

Pacific Flounder: Usually incor-rectly marketed as turbot, the Pacific flounder does not live up to its eastern cousin.

Fluke: Also *summer flounder.* The fluke ranges in size from 3 to 5 pounds and is usually sold in fillet form.

Brill: This European fish is like turbot, but is not as flavorful.

Yellowtail Flounder: Also more commonly sold simply as "floun-der," this variety is lean and fairly tasty.

GRAYLING

Other Names and Species: Alaska grayling, American grayling, Montana grayling

Freshwater

This game fish is becoming more and more rare. It was once quite abundant in this country, but has been driven north up to Canada and Alaska. It is said to smell like thyme, from which it derives its Latin name, *thymus.* It is in the same family as trout and salmon, and it resembles them in flavor. It is, unfortunately, available only to those who catch their own.

GROUPER

See under Bass

HADDOCK

See under Cod

HAKE

See under Cod

HALIBUT

Other Names and Species: Atlantic halibut, California halibut, chicken halibut, Pacific halibut

Saltwater/Atlantic and Pacific

The halibut is the largest member of the bottom-dwelling flatfish family, of which sole and flounder are members. Our name for halibut comes from the Middle English word *halybutte, haly* mean-ing "holy," and *butte* meaning "fish." The "holyfish," or halibut, was traditionally the fish eaten on Christian holy days. Like other bottom-dwellers, the halibut has both eyes on top and will burrow its flat body on the sandy ocean bottom when in danger. That's impressive for a fish that weighs up to 300 pounds!

The Atlantic halibut can grow to be quite enormous. It has firm white meat, and is usually sold as steaks or fillets. The Pacific halibut is similar in flavor, which is quite good, but is not much larger that 12 pounds. It may be found whole, pan-dressed, steaked, or filleted. California halibut is similar to but not as flavorful as the other halibuts.

The halibut has a very mild flavor, and it is relatively lean. It must not be overcooked or the result is dry, uninteresting fish. Poaching, baking, or broiling with a basting sauce is recommended, and it combines well with many sauces.

HERRING
Other Names and Species: Alewife, blueback, kipper, pilchard, sardine, sprat
Saltwater/Atlantic and Pacific

The herring was once an extremely important international commodity, much like oil is today. Wars were fought among European countries over herring spawning waters, the control of which could determine a country's economic destiny.

Herring is oily and relatively small. It is not popular in this country in fresh form, though it is often seen in one of its many prepared forms. Fresh herring is wonderful grilled, since its oily flesh keeps it quite moist and tender. It is also often pan-fried or smoked.

A kipper is a cured and smoked herring, though the word "kippered" has come to be synonymous with "smoked." Herring is also sold pickled, creamed, brined, smoked, and as sardines.

JACK FISH
Other Names and Species: Amberjack, ulua, *yellow jack, yellowtail*
Saltwater/Atlantic and Pacific

Jack fish are not a particularly popular food fish in the United States except in Hawaii, where they are called *ulua*. They are mild-tasting, with delicate flavor and texture. The jack fish yellowtail is well known to those who frequent *sushi* bars, however, as a delicious, sweet fish with a smooth texture. Jack fish adapt well to nearly any cooking method, and are excellent grilled.

JOHN DORY
Other Names and Species: St. Peter's fish, St. Pierre
Saltwater/Atlantic

The john dory is not a common market fish, but its flavor is delightful. The fish is nicknamed for St. Peter because of the legend surrounding its markings. The fish has two large round yellow-outlined black spots on either side of its body near the head. It is said that Peter was instructed by Jesus to capture a fish and look in its mouth, where he would find a coin to distribute to the people. According to the story, Peter held the fish so tightly in his search that he left his fingerprints.

The john dory is a firm fish with a fine flake, not unlike sole. It is generally small enough to pan-fry, or to sauté in fillet form.

LINGCOD
Other Names and Species: Buffalo cod, greenling, rock cod
Saltwater/Pacific

The lingcod is *not* a cod. The "ling" half of the name points to its real origin: the greenling family. These fish have slender bodies, with sharp teeth lining a large mouth. The lingcod is distinguished by a slightly green-tinted flesh that turns white when cooked. The lingcod is a firm, lean fish and tends to dry out if overcooked. It has a mild, unassertive flavor and dense flesh. It can be grilled or broiled with a basting sauce or marinade, poached, or used in stews and soups.

LOBSTER
Other Names and Species: American lobster, European lobster, homard, langoustine, lobsterette, Maine lobster, rock lobster, scampo, spiny lobster
Saltwater/Atlantic and Pacific

Most people, even those who aren't particularly fond of seafood, have a place reserved in their heart for lobster. Lobster is in a special category of its own. It is served in the most elegant restaurants and the most humble fish shanties. It can be eaten with tiny forks or the fingers. Regardless of how it's eaten, the lobster is one of America's favorite crustaceans. We can only hope we don't eat it all up.

In the late 1800s, lobster was still so abundant in New England that it was used as bait for such fish as cod. The ability to transport live lobster has been a mixed blessing: on the one hand folks from other parts of the country can enjoy it without having to travel to Maine. On the other hand the boom in consumption has reduced the overall lobster population, and we harvest them now when they are much smaller, thus cutting those reproductive years off the life of the lobster.

Lobster is delicious boiled or steamed, or basted with a flavored butter and grilled or broiled. The coral, or roe, of the female is delicious in sauces or compound butters, as is the green soft matter called the tomalley, or liver.

American Lobster: Also *Maine lobster.* This is the lobster of Maine fame. It is more commonly called a Maine lobster, but that isn't necessarily where it will have come from. Lobster is associated with Maine since that is where the first commercial lobster fishery was started, but in recent years the actual number taken from Maine shores has been drastically reduced. The American lobster is usually harvested at 1 to 5 pounds, although they would grow larger than that if allowed to. The average size for one serving is 1 to 1½ pounds. They are reddish-brown, often speckled, with two types of claws: the "crusher claw," which is the large one and is used for that purpose, and the "quick claw" for small ripping and tearing jobs. Lobsters eat a lot of small shellfish, and hide out in the dark corners of rocky shores.

Spiny Lobster: Also *rock lobster.* Spiny lobsters come from the warm waters of the tropics and subtropics, so the ones we see are imported. The "spines" referred to in their name are their two long antennae, which they use as weapons because they have no claws. Therefore, the meat is all from the tail. Spiny lobster has a slightly coarser texture than the American lobster, but excellent flavor. It is generally marketed as frozen tails.

Lobsterette: Also *scampo, langoustine.* Known best in the dish called *scampi,* this tiny lobster is related to the larger varieties. A lobsterette is all tail meat, however, and because of its small size and shape it has often been confused with or replaced by the shrimp. It is, however, a lobster.

To select live lobster: Pick lobsters that are lively in the tank. The claws should be strapped or pegged since lobsters are carnivorous and will eat each other if left alone. The shells should be hard. Size is unrelated to flavor, though some people claim the huge ones are tough. The female lobsters are meatier and contain the coral (roe); they can be distinguished by their wider abdomen and the soft set of swimmerets at the junction of the body and the tail (on the male they are hard).

To Kill a Live Lobster: There are a number of ways to kill a lobster, but we feel the best way is to plunge it into boiling water for 1 minute. This is a more certain and probably more humane method than attempting to sever its spinal cord. Run the lobster under cool water to stop the cooking process.

To Remove Raw Meat: Kill the lobster (see above). Cut down the under shell of the tail from the body end to the tail (scissors or kitchen shears are best for this), and remove the meat. Remove the gray instestinal tract and discard. Cut up through the body, and remove and reserve the coral (if any) and tomalley. Crack the claws and remove the meat, and remove any meat that remains in the body section.

To Dress a Whole Lobster: Kill the lobster (see above). Cut down the under shell of the tail from the body end to the tail, cutting either all the way through the hard shell or only through the under shell to the meat. Cut up through the body. Remove the gray intestinal tract that runs down to the tail and discard. Remove the coral (if any) and tomalley and reserve. Remove and discard the gill tissues, sand sac, and any other non-meat matter in the body. To butterfly: Cut all the way through the hard shell of the tail up to the body. Each tail half can be curled upwards toward the claws to expose more meat, or the tail can be spread apart. To split: Cut all the way through the

hard tail shell as well as the body, for two equal halves. To fan cut: Cut away the soft under shell along its edges to fully expose the meat, but leave the hard shell intact.

To Cook Lobster: Drop live lobsters into boiling salted water (⅓ cup salt per gallon of water). When the water returns to a boil, cook, covered, for 8 to 10 minutes for a 1-pound lobster, adding 5 minutes per each additional pound. Don't overcrowd the kettle. Grill or broil dressed lobster with a basting sauce until the meat is opaque and tender and the shell is bright red.

To Select Precooked Lobster: The tail of the lobster is the best indication of its freshness: it should be curled under the lobster and snap back into the curled position when extended.

MACKEREL

Other Names and Species: Atlantic mackerel, blue mackerel, Boston mackerel, cero, chub, king, ono, sierra, Spanish, tinker, wahoo

Saltwater/Atlantic and Pacific

Mackerel is related to tuna and shares some of its characteristics, such as oily rich flesh and a dark band of musculature. The mackerel has been underplayed in this country, perhaps because its flavor is considered somewhat exotic. But it is delicious grilled, especially if marinated in a lemon or lime marinade for half an hour before cooking to cut some of its oiliness. It has a fine texture, and its grayish meat cooks to white.

The wahoo is considered to be the top-of-the-line mackerel. In Hawaii it is called *ono,* or "sweet," and not without reason. The Spanish, cero, and king are also known for their good texture and flavor. A tinker is generally considered a juvenile mackerel. The best season for mackerel is late spring through early summer. It is usually sold whole, pan-dressed, or filleted. The dark band of muscle may be removed, as its flavor is stronger, but this is optional.

MAHI-MAHI
See under Dolphinfish

MONKFISH
See under Angler

MULLET
Other Names and Species: Black mullet, gray mullet, lisa, red mullet, silver mullet, striped mullet, white mullet

Saltwater/Atlantic

Mullet abounds in many of the world's oceans, but only a few species are palatable. In the United States, mullet is only moderately popular, and the most important are the silver and striped mullets. Red mullet is really a goatfish, and has all white meat of delicate texture, unlike the true mullets. The mullet has a portion of dark meat, and relatively firm, fatty flesh. It is quite tasty grilled or broiled because of its high fat content. It also has a notably high protein and mineral content.

MUSSEL
Other Names and Species: Bay mussel, blue mussel, California mussel, edible mussel, green mussel, green-lipped mussel, moule

Saltwater/Atlantic and Pacific

The blue mussel is by far the most common mussel in American waters. It is abundant in New England and California, where they grow in the wild and are also cultivated. Mussels cling to their beds with long, grasslike fibers, which become the "beard" that hangs off the mussel once it is harvested. A.J. McClane, in *The Encyclopedia of Fish Cookery,* explains that the mussel secretes this fiber, which firms up on contact with salt water. He says that ancient Greek fishermen collected the fibers and wove them into gloves to protect their hands. The gloves had to be kept in salt water to keep them from drying up or withering away. The strength and durability of the fiber was so great that the gloves were handed down from father to son for many generations.

Blue mussels are a very dark blue with smooth shells. California mussels are larger, and the large green-lipped mussel (usually from New Zealand) has a distinctive green edge. Purchase mussels from a reputable fishmonger, as they are subject to seasonal prohibition on the West Coast (see "Red Tide," page 43).

Mussels are quite good for you. They contain over 10 percent protein and under 3 percent fat.

They are rich in vitamins as well. Always buy more mussels than you need since a few won't open after cooking. Buy about 1 pound per person.

To Select Live Mussels: All mussels should be alive when you cook them (unless they are smoked or precooked). Avoid any mussels that are broken or open, or that will not close when the muscle is pricked with the tip of a knife. Overly light or heavy mussels should be avoided, as the first ones may be dead and the second full of sand. Hold each mussel between your thumb and forefinger, and push it gently on the bias. A live muscle will stay tightly closed, while dead ones will break apart easily.

To Clean, Soak, and Debeard Mussels: Clean and debeard mussels shortly before cooking. Pull off the beard by holding it and yanking it firmly. Scrub the mussels under running water with a vegetable brush, or agitate them in a sink full of water to allow the shells to rub against each other. Soak the mussels for an hour in lightly salted water, ⅓ cup of salt per gallon of water.

To Cook Mussels: Mussels are usually steamed until they open in water, wine, or a combination of these. Discard any that do not open.

OCTOPUS
Other Names and Species: Devilfish, pulpo
Saltwater/Atlantic and Pacific

This admittedly unattractive creature is not the monster Hollywood has tried to make it. It is actually a rather shy and retiring shellfish that is rarely the size of the giants on *Voyage to the Bottom of the Sea*. It is a mollusk and, like the squid, a cephalopod. It is most common in the Pacific. Eight tentacles with suction cups hang from its round body, and they are often white tipped with burgundy. The octopus eats mollusks and crustaceans, and therefore has very sweet and flavorful meat that is much undervalued.

Octopus is delicious grilled, broiled, or stewed, but it must be tenderized before cooking by simmering it for 45 minutes or by pounding slices well with a wooden mallet. To clean an octopus, turn it inside out, cut around

the yellow sac, and pull it out. The viscera will come with it. Rinse well.

ORANGE ROUGHY
Saltwater/Pacific

The orange roughy is a newcomer to the American dinner table. It is from New Zealand, where it was "discovered" and from whence it has come since 1979. It is actually a variety of ocean perch, a relative of the rockfish. Its firm white meat is rather mild-tasting and can be prepared by almost any cooking method.

Orange roughy is flash-frozen at sea, so don't refreeze it once it's home. The texture is excellent, though, considering it has been frozen.

OYSTER
Other Names and Species: See below
Saltwater/Atlantic and Pacific

The belief that oysters increase sexual potency is an ancient one. Though it has not been proven, it's nice to believe, because there is no denying that eating raw oysters is sensuous. The Romans certainly thought so when they cultivated them over two thousand years ago. The oyster's high protein content may be the source of any extra energy they supposedly supply.

Oysters live in bays and at the mouths of rivers where there is a certain amount of fresh water mixed with the salt water. Oysters in the wild are subject to "red tide" (see page 43), though the farmed variety are carefully monitored. Purchase oysters from a reliable fishmonger. Oysters will stay alive up to one week—not from the time you bought them but from the time they were gathered, so keep that in mind when you store them. Store oysters in the fridge loosely covered with the cup side down for no more than two days. Don't soak or store oysters in water.

Oysters are usually served raw on the half shell or in stew, but they are delicious grilled in the shell as well. Place unopened oysters on the grill cup side down; when they pop open, twist off the top shell, add a little flavored

butter, and put them back on the grill until the butter just begins to sizzle. Oysters are also available shucked and stored in jars, dried, or smoked.

Atlantic Oysters: The varieties available from Atlantic waters, where most of the best oysters come from, are Blue Point or Long Island Blue Point, Chesapeake, Chincoteague, Cotuit, Belon or plate, Apalachicola, Kent Island, New Orleans, Malpeque, and Wellfleet.

Pacific Oysters: Belon or plate, Hawaiian, Japanese or Pacific, Olympia, Tomales Bay, and Walapa Bay. Oysters are more flavorful when grown in colder waters, so among Pacific oysters, the northern ones tend to be better.

To Select Live Oysters: Avoid open and abnormally light shells. Shells should be tightly closed. Shucked oysters packed in jars should be plump and in very clear liquor.

To Shuck Oysters: Shuck oysters over a bowl to collect any spilled liquor. Hold the oyster in your hand, cup side down and level, with a mitt or towel. Using an oyster knife (a screwdriver may be used also), work the tip between the shells very near the hinge. Slide it in sideways and work it a little way around the edge of the shell. Do not puncture the muscle. Twist and pry upward until you hear a crack. Slide the knife in and sever the top connector muscle. Pry off the top shell. Remove any shell bits. Spoon extra liquor into the bottom shell if needed. Sever the bottom connector muscle and serve on the half shell.

PERCH
Other Names and Species: Dore, walleye, walleye pike, white perch, yellow perch
Freshwater

Perch are small freshwater fish, usually caught by amateur fishermen and pan-fried the same day. Thus they are almost never seen in fish markets. The perches have white, usually firm flesh, and are sweet and fresh-tasting. Yellow and white perch are the most abundant in American waters. The walleye, also called a dore or walleye pike (incorrectly, since it's not a pike), has naturally cloudy eyes, an exception to the rule that fresh fish must have clear eyes. It has fine flakes and is quite tasty.

PERIWINKLE

Other Names and Species: Winkles

Saltwater and Freshwater/ Atlantic and Pacific

The periwinkle is one of the sea snails, together with the abalone, whelk, and conch. The small shell is a cone-shaped spiral, often brightly marked or colored, and usually no bigger than 1 inch. Winkles are delicious boiled and dipped in butter, like clams. Scrub the shells under cold running water. Place in salted water to cover and bring to a boil. Cook for 5 minutes. With a small knife, cut the muscle that attaches to the shell. Pick out the meat with a toothpick.

PIKE

Other Names and Species: Blackspotted pike, blue pike, grass pike, great pike, muskellunge, pickerel, sauger, silver pike

Freshwater

The pike is a rather odd-looking fish with a duck-billed nose and a long body. Most pike is caught by fishermen rather than fished commercially, and it is rarely seen in the market. It has mild, sweet meat with a flaky texture, and is low in fat. The pickerel is a small pike.

PLAICE

See under Flounder

POLLOCK

See under Cod

POMPANO

Other Names and Species: Palometa, permit, sunfish

Saltwater/Atlantic and Pacific

These silvery fish are flat as pancakes. They zip over the top of the water, slapping down on the surface to gain momentum, and flashing in the sun. The permit is larger than the pompano, and although it is not a true pompano, it is very similar in flavor and texture. Pompano has firm, flavorful white meat. It is considered to be a delicacy, which its price reflects.

Pompano are quite small, though fillets from the largest ones are available. Smaller pompano are sold whole, pan-dressed, or butterflied. They are good broiled, grilled, or sautéed.

PORGY

Other Names and Species: Dorade, mu, northern porgy, Pacific porgy, red porgy, scup, sea bream

Saltwater/Atlantic and Pacific

The porgy most likely derives its interesting name from the Narragansett Indian word *mishcuppaoug* (*mishe* meaning "thick," and *cuppi* meaning "scaled.") The word was later shortened to *scuppaug*, and New Englanders used the first half, *scup*, for the fish, while New Yorkers took the second half, *paug*, and changed it to *paugie* or *porgy*. At any rate, the Indian name is accurate, because the porgy is known for its tough skin and thick scales. It has lean, coarsely textured flesh, but very good flavor. The smaller fish are more complicated to bone, so select large ones from a range of 1½ to 2 pounds. Porgy is well suited to the grill.

PRAWN

See under Shrimp

REDFISH

See under Drum and Rockfish

RED SNAPPER

See under Snapper

ROCKFISH

Other Names and Species: Black snapper, boccacio, canary, ocean perch, Pacific ocean perch, Pacific snapper, priestfish, quillback, redfish, red snapper, rock cod, striped bass, vermillion, yellowtail

Saltwater/Atlantic and Pacific

The rockfish family is quite large and includes over 250 varieties. The rockfish generally has good flavor and a firm but tender texture. Despite the things it has going for it, however, the rockfish is more often marketed under a pseudonym than under its own name. Because there are so many varieties, many resemble *other* types of fish, some of them more valuable, so that rockfish can be marketed at the higher price. The most common example of this is the Pacific red snapper. Red snapper is *not* a Pacific fish, though it would appear to be if you judge by its abundance in the market. What is abundant in the Pacific, however, is a variety of rockfish that looks like the red snapper. Red snapper from the East Coast will be marked "true red snapper." The rock cod is not a cod but a rockfish. And a perfectly good one. The ocean perch is the least characteristic rockfish, and is often treated as a separate species.

Rockfish can be cooked in almost any way. They are usually steamed whole in Chinese cuisine—be careful of the sharp spines on the fins and the gill covers.

SABLEFISH

Other Names and Species: Black cod, butterfish, coal fish, skil

Saltwater/Pacific

Sablefish is the butterfish of the West Coast. It comes from the very cold northern waters of the Pacific, and is usually sold smoked. Its oily white flesh is mild, soft-textured, and best suited for smoking, but it can be broiled or grilled as well.

SALMON

Other Names and Species: Atlantic, chinook, chum, coho, humpback, king, pink, red, silver, sockeye

Freshwater and Saltwater/ Atlantic and Pacific

Salmon is unmistakable, both in flavor and in color. It has bright orange to red flesh, a delicious, rich flavor, a delicate flake, and firm, dense flesh. It can be prepared nearly any way with great success. The salmon has been appreciated for thousands of years: salmon bones and cave paintings of the fish have been found in Stone Age caves. America at one time had so much salmon that they glutted the rivers and streams during spawning season. Due to overfishing and pollution, salmon populations are now greatly reduced, particularly on the East Coast.

Salmon comes whole, pandressed, steaked, filleted, canned, brined, and smoked.

Chinook: Also *king*. The chinook is considered to be the best of the salmon. It is the largest (up to 15 or 20 pounds), and has tender meat and a rich flavor due to its somewhat high fat content. It is a Pacific salmon.

Coho: Also *silver*. The coho is also a delicious salmon, though a bit leaner and considerably smaller. It is also from the Pacific.

Atlantic: This salmon is nearly gone, but efforts are being made to restore it.

ROCKFISH

Bonito

Coho Salmon

Sockeye: Also *red*. Sockeye is good, though not as flavorful as the chinook or coho. The flesh of the sockeye is quite red.

Chum: This salmon is most often smoked or used for canning.

Humpback: Also *pink*. Humpback is almost always canned.

Lox: Lox is mild, salt-cured salmon that used to be made from the Atlantic salmon. It was popularized by the Russian Jewish community in London in the nineteenth century, and was introduced to America by Jewish immigrants. It is now made from Pacific salmon.

Nova: Nova may have originated in Nova Scotia, but today it is a cold-smoked salmon made in New York from Pacific salmon.

SAND DAB
See under Flounder

SARDINE
Other Names and Species: Atlantic sardine, blueback, bugfish, pilchard, sprat

Saltwater/Atlantic and Pacific

Sardines are any small fish from the herring family (see under Herring), but the term usually applies to small salted fish packed into tins. Canning sardines originated in Sardinia, off the coast of Italy, as a way of preserving large catches of these small fish.

SCALLOP
Other Names and Species: Bay scallop, calico, coquille St. Jacques, rock scallop, sea scallop

Saltwater/Atlantic and Pacific

The best way in the world to eat a scallop is right from a shell you have just plucked from the sea. But because scallops do not hold their shells tightly closed, they die very quickly out of water, which is why most scallops we see in the market are already shucked. Scallops have a rounded symmetrical shell with evenly-spaced ribs (made familiar by the gas station logo). They move freely in the water by shooting out a jet of water that propels them up to a yard.

Fresh scallops should be cream-colored or ivory, not gray or pure white. Though they are almost never sold with the scallop, the roe is quite delicious. Scallops have in the past been "created" from skate wings, but this has been prohibited. Also in the past, Bay scallops may have been stamped out of the larger sea scallops, but this has become economically unnecessary, since sea scallops now command an equally high price.

Scallops have a sweet, very delicate flavor, and a smooth velvety texture. They should be cooked very briefly, only until they lose their translucency. They are delicious sautéed, broiled, or skewered and grilled over hot coals.

Bay Scallop: This is the smallest scallop, and comes from the East Coast.

Calico: Though often sold as a bay scallop, the calico is not quite as rich or flavorful. Most calicoes are harvested in Florida.

Sea Scallop: This large scallop grows up to 1½ inches in diameter.

Rock Scallop: From the Pacific Coast, these are the largest scallops.

SCROD
See under Cod

SEA BASS
See under Bass

SEA URCHIN
Saltwater/Atlantic and Pacific

This prickly, unapproachable creature yields a delectable roe considered by many cultures to be quite a delicacy. The sea urchin is a small round ball covered with spines, found most often (and all too often by unwitting bathers) in tide pools and reefs and along shallow shorelines. The roe (actually the gonads) is a dull yellowish-orange mass—the only edible part of the sea urchin. The Japanese prize the sea urchin, or *uni,* for use in *sushi.* It can be found shelled in Japanese fish markets.

Wear gloves when collecting your own sea urchins. They must be ripe, which occurs during the colder months: late fall through early spring. Cut a hole around the bottom, or mouth, shake out the viscera, and spoon out the yellow mass clinging to the top. This yellow mass is the edible roe.

SHAD
Other Names and Species: American shad, white shad

Freshwater and Saltwater/ Atlantic

This silver-speckled fish is the largest member of the herring family. It lives in salt water but will swim into eastern rivers to spawn, at which time it is usually fished. The female contains the highly regarded roe, which can be prepared in a number of ways. Shad has a complicated bone structure with two rows of ribs, and often filleting is the best way to solve this problem.

Shad is delicious grilled or broiled, or poached with sorrel. The roe (with the outer membrane removed) should be parboiled for 5 minutes in salted water before proceeding with preparation. It can then be baked, broiled, sautéed, grilled, or chopped for mousse.

SHARK
Other Names and Species: Blacktip shark, blue shark, dogfish, leopard shark, mako shark, soupfin shark, spiny dogfish, thresher shark, tiger shark

Saltwater/Atlantic and Pacific

The traditional association of shark with danger kept it off the dinner table for many years. Recently, however, shark has gained popularity and is commanding a rather high price. One reason for its popularity is that is has only one central bone. Also, it is low in fat and very firm. The meat should be marinated or basted, however, to keep it moist.

Shark does have one unusual feature that requires a little advance preparation. Because it relies on its metabolism to maintain the proper balance of salt and water (sharks have no gills to do this), the flesh contains a high concentration of urea. This has the odor of ammonia, and though it is entirely harmless, it may be off-putting. Time diminishes the odor, so a slightly less fresh cut will hardly have any. Soak shark in a solution of water and lemon or vinegar, or in just plain milk for an hour. The skin should always be removed, as it shrinks when cooked and will distort the fish.

The mako shark is the most common shark on the East Coast, while the thresher is the West Coast preference. Shark is almost always sold as steaks.

SHRIMP

Other Names and Species: Crevette, Bay shrimp, brown shrimp, grass shrimp, kuruma prawn, Monterey prawn, pink shrimp, prawn, rock shrimp, scampi, sea-bob, spot shrimp, tiger prawn, white shrimp

Freshwater and Saltwater/ Atlantic and Pacific

The shrimp is a very abundant creature in the United States, and is our most valuable commercial seafood. The distinction between "shrimp" and "prawn" is one that has been debated, but the proper difference is simply that shrimp are sea creatures while prawns dwell in fresh water. Prawns are sweeter and more perishable than shrimp, and they generally come from Hawaii and Asia. However, large shrimp are commonly referred to as *prawns.* The size range of shrimp is, indeed, impressive: from 300 per pound to 3 per pound. The usual size breakdown is as follows:
Jumbo (or Prawn): Under 10 per pound
Large (or Prawn): 10 to 25 per pound
Medium: 25 to 40 per pound
Small: 40 to 60 per pound
Tiny: Over 60 per pound

Shrimp are available raw (or "green"); heads on or off; frozen; cooked and shelled or unshelled; smoked; canned; as paste; and dried. "Scampi" are not shrimp but lobsterettes (see under Lobster), though the dish is often prepared with shrimp and called Shrimp Scampi.

To Select Fresh Shrimp: Select firm and sweet-smelling shrimp, with the shells well attached. Stale shrimp have a slight ammonia odor. Raw shrimp with the heads on deteriorate more quickly, so cook them the same day you purchase them.

To Shell and Devein Shrimp: Snap off the head. Pull off the shell, leaving the tail shell on, if desired. The dark, stringlike vein along the back may be removed, but this is optional. The vein is harmless, but it is often removed for aesthetic reasons. Deveining is not worth the effort with small shrimp, or shrimp that will be cooked in the shell. To remove the vein, gently cut a shallow "V" along the back and scrape the vein out with a paring knife. You may also use a shrimp deveiner.

SKATE

Other Names and Species: Big skate, California skate, flapper skate, ray, winter skate

Saltwater/Atlantic and Pacific

The skate, or ray, is a flat diamond-shaped creature with wings and a whiplike tail—most alarming-looking in its natural habitat. Skates eat mollusks, though, which gives them an excellent flavor that is underappreciated in this country. Only the wings are edible, and the flavor has been compared to scallops. Skate actually becomes more tender if held in the refrigerator for a few days before cooking it.

Skate wings should be skinned and soaked in water with lemon juice or vinegar for several hours before cooking. The most common cooking method is poaching.

SMELT

Other Names and Species: Candlefish, capelin, Columbia River smelt, eperlan, jacksmelt, rainbow smelt, silversides, sparling, surf smelt, whitebait

Freshwater and Saltwater/ Atlantic and Pacific

Smelts are small fish related to the herring family. They are often the fish used in whitebait, a dish of deep-fried small juvenile fish. The average length of the smelt is about 6 inches, and they are sold whole, gutted, or pan-dressed. Smelts are best dusted with flour, pan-fried, and eaten with the fingers.

SNAPPER

Other Names and Species: Gray snapper, mutton snapper, red snapper, silver snapper, vermillion snapper

Saltwater/Atlantic

Snappers are lean and firm with pinkish-tinted flesh. Their flavor is excellent—slightly sweet yet unassertive. There are a number of snappers, but by far the most common one is the red snapper. On the West Coast, rockfish is often marketed as red snapper or Pacific red snapper, but the real thing should be labeled "true red snapper." Red snappers have bright-red eyes and are completely red in color, and their average size is between 2 and 10 pounds. Other snappers are also available and may be marketed as red snapper.

Their flavor and texture are very similar. Red snapper is most commonly sold in fillet form.

SOLE

Other Names and Species: Butter sole, channel sole, Dover sole, English sole, French sole, gray sole, lemon sole, petrale sole, rex sole, sand sole

Saltwater/Atlantic and Pacific

Ancient Rome named this fish for what it looked like to them: *solea,* the sole of a sandal. The sole is one of the three members of the large family of flatfish, which includes flounder and halibut. The sole is the most flavorful of the flatfish, however, and has the finest texture. As evidence of its versatility, there are over three hundred recipes in classic French cuisine for sole alone. Unfortunately, the fish we call "sole" in this country is really flounder rather than true sole. We do have, however, some very impressive runners-up.

Our sole can be prepared following any cooking method, and it goes well with almost any sauce. Sole should be grilled on a piece of perforated aluminum foil and not turned.

Dover Sole: 1. A common European sole. 2. A Pacific flounder of good quality, but not as delicate as the petrale or sand soles.
Petrale Sole: A large Pacific flounder, generally rated the best among the sole substitutes. It is almost always sold in fillet form.
Sand Sole: A smaller Pacific flounder, rated second to the petrale in quality. Sold pan-dressed or filleted.
Rex Sole: Very small Pacific flounder with a fine texture. These tend to be pricey since they are less often available. Usually sold pan-dressed and skinned.
Butter Sole: A good Pacific flounder that ranks just a bit below the petrale and sand soles.
Gray Sole: An Atlantic flounder of good quality, well known on the East Coast.
English Sole: A moderately good Pacific flounder.

SPRAT

See under Herring

Swordfish

Shark

Tuna

SQUID

Other Names and Species: Calamari, *cuttlefish, market squid*

Saltwater/Pacific

The squid is altogether an odd shellfish. It has no shell except for the long plasticlike quill *inside* its body. It, like the octopus, is a cephalopod, literally a head with feet. The squid also has its own strange form of self-defense: it carries an ink sac from which it can squirt a dark substance to "smoke screen" the enemy and make its getaway. The squid swims in schools and feeds nocturnally on all types of fish (even other squid). It is plentiful, and is an efficient food source, since over 80 percent of it is edible. It has very lean meat that contains about 17 percent protein.

The squid is pearly white with purple skin. It has a delicious, mild flavor and a slightly chewy texture. If overcooked squid becomes downright tough. But it is excellent pan-fried, sautéed, stir-fried, grilled, deep-fried, baked, stuffed, used in stews, or broiled. It is sold whole, cleaned, in steaks, or frozen in blocks. Large squid steaks should be pounded with a mallet to tenderize, unless the fishmonger has done this.

To Clean Fresh Squid: (See above for illustration.) Once in the swing of it, cleaning squid is really quite simple. Pull the head and tentacles away from the body. The viscera will come out with the head. Cut the tentacles off just below the eye (this being the tentacle side of the eye rather than the viscera side). Discard the head and viscera. Pop the small round beak (a pea-sized hard part) out of the tentacles and discard. Pull out the long quill, the transparent piece inside the body, and discard. Scrape the outside of the body with the dull side of a knife to press out remaining matter. This may have been broken into 2 or 3 pieces, so be sure to remove it all. The purplish skin may be pulled or scraped off. Leaving it on adds flavor, but may make a white sauce slightly purple. Rinse the body and tentacles and pat dry.

STRIPED BASS

See under Bass

STURGEON

Other Names and Species: Beluga, green *sturgeon, hackleback, shortnose, white sturgeon*

Freshwater and Saltwater/ Pacific

Sturgeon is most famous for its contribution of caviar to the world. The fish itself, however, is quite tasty. It has firm, fairly rich meat that is relatively high in fat. It is often smoked, and when fresh is best suited to the grill or broiler.

SUCKER

Other Names and Species: Bigmouth *buffalo, blue sucker, buffalofish, redhorse sucker, spotted sucker, white sucker*

Freshwater

The sucker earned its name from its peculiar eating habit, which resembles vacuuming. Its rounded, protruding lips that point downward in a pout facilitate this sucking action on lake and river bottoms. And rather than stopping to chew (since they don't have teeth), the bones in their throats do all the grinding necessary. The buffaloes are the most popular of the suckers, since they have the fewest bones. Buffaloes have a mild, freshwater flavor and a relatively firm texture.

SUNFISH

Other Names and Species: Bluegill, *bream, crappie, flier, redear, rock bass, warmouth*

Freshwater

Sunfish are an extremely abundant variety of freshwater fish caught almost exclusively by amateur fishermen. They are tasty little fish that should be eaten the day they are caught, preferably dusted with a little cornmeal and pan-fried. The lean meat of the sunfish is slightly sweet and fresh-tasting. The skin is edible and in fact quite good. It adds flavor and holds in moisture.

SURIMI

Surimi is an imitation shellfish meat made from processed Alaska or walleye pollock. It is most often seen as imitation crab meat (often called "krab") or shrimp meat. Surimi is overprocessed and over-salted.

SWORDFISH

Other Names and Species: Broadbill, *spearfish*

Saltwater/Atlantic and Pacific

The swordfish is known the world over, not so much for its meat but for its physique. It carries on its nose a long, dangerous sword, with which it can wreak much havoc. The swordfish has been known to attack small (and large!) boats and floating objects, not to mention the damage it does to its prey. But swordfish is delicious eating and has excellent flavor. New fishing methods have made it possible to capture the swordfish more efficiently than before, so it makes its way to the market with more regularity.

Swordfish has an almost beeflike flavor. The meat is firm, dense, and slightly oily. It is best grilled or broiled, especially if marinated first or basted while cooking. Don't overcook swordfish, as it easily becomes dry and loses flavor.

TILEFISH
Other Names and Species: Golden snapper, tile bass, white snapper
Saltwater/Atlantic

The tilefish is much like the angler in flavor. It, too, feeds on small crustaceans such as crabs and shrimp, and mollusks as well. The tilefish has firm, sweet meat that has been compared to lobster. It is quite versatile, and can be prepared almost any way. It combines well with many sauces, and is excellent in fish soups.

TROUT
Other Names and Species: See below
Freshwater and Saltwater

The trout is one of this country's most preferred fish. It has a delightful flavor—not too assertive, mildly sweet—and a fine, moist texture. It is easy to bone, raw or cooked, and has virtually no scales, which endears it to many people. Fishing for trout is very high on the list of outdoor activities for American leisure time. However, it is also one of our most "farmed" fish.

Trout caught in the wild are superior to the farmed variety, primarily because of the wild trout's diet. Fishermen also claim that the more a trout has to fight, the better its flavor, which puts the farm trout, with its sluggish, easy life, fairly low on the taste scale. But the farmed varieties are still quite good, and are certainly worth eating between fishing trips.

Trout is excellent pan-fried, grilled, poached, baked, or broiled. The skin is delicious and should be left on. Trout is usually sold pan-dressed or butterflied.

Look particularly for freshness when buying trout (see page 37).

Rainbow Trout: Rainbow trout are the best-known trout in the market. Any rainbow you see in a store will be the cultivated variety, and though their flavor is good, it doesn't quite match that of the wild rainbow trout. They are distinguished by their bright side stripes and speckled silver skin.

Brook Trout: The brook trout from the wild has pale yellowish-orange flesh, while farmed brook trout will have white flesh. They are excellent eating, particularly those taken from mountain streams. The brook trout has red spots and a red stomach.

Brown Trout: The brown trout is also excellent eating. Though it is mostly caught by sport fishermen, there is limited farming of this variety of trout. It is brown with large dark spots.

Char: Chars are not trout, but they are similar. They come from very cold northern waters, and are most often seen smoked in the markets. The Dolly Varden and the lake trout are chars.

Cutthroat: The cutthroat is named for the red slash mark at its neck, which stands out against its brown spotted skin. These trout are delicious, but mostly the fare of fishermen who catch their own.

Golden Trout: This is a high-mountain-stream trout of excellent quality. It has yellow skin and orange flesh.

Steelhead: Steelheads are the sea-run variety of the rainbow trout, and they are a bit larger. They are quite delicious, with a flavor somewhere between trout and salmon.

TUNA
Other Names and Species: Ahi, albacore, bigeye, blackfin tuna, bluefin tuna, bonito, longfin tuna, skipjack tuna, tunny fish, yellowfin tuna
Saltwater/Atlantic and Pacific

The tuna is one of the larger edible fish in the sea, with the huge bluefin able to achieve a weight of up to 1,500 pounds. But 1,500 pounds of fish is very difficult to manage, so most bluefins are caught at around 300 pounds, or about 12 feet long. Unfortunately, tuna is better known in its cooked and canned form. Of the canned tunas, the albacore is prime qual-

ity, the only one allowed to be labeled "white meat" tuna.

The meat of all tuna is red when raw and turns white when cooked. The dark strip of muscle has a more intense flavor, and may be removed. The tuna is an oily, rich-tasting fish, best broiled or grilled. Overcooking it tends to make it dry. Tuna is delicious cold.

Albacore: The albacore is a small tuna of good quality with light-colored meat. It is favored by the canning industry.

Bigeye: Bigeyes are quite large, and are good eating. The bigeye is popular in Japanese cuisine, particularly for *sushi*.

Blackfin: This tuna is not too well known in American markets, but is a light-fleshed variety with good flavor.

Bluefin: The bluefin has darkish meat, but good flavor.

Yellowfin: Also *Ahi*. A very common tuna in both Atlantic and Pacific waters, this tuna has very good flavor.

Bonito: The bonito has very oily, very dark flesh, but its rich flavor is the prized *katsuo* in Japanese *sushi*. The skipjack tuna is very similar to the bonito.

TURBOT
See under Flounder

WAHOO
See under Mackerel

WALLEYE
See under Perch

WEAKFISH
See under Drum

WHELK
Other Names and Species: Scungilli, sea snail
Saltwater/Atlantic

The whelk is very similar to the periwinkle, and is related to the conch and abalone as well. Whelks are best known in the Italian dish *scungilli,* but are also used in stews or chowders. Whelks must be cooked slowly to tenderize them. To remove them from the shell, place them in a pot of salted water and bring to a boil. Boil gently for 3 minutes. Remove the meat and slice off the viscera.

WHITEBAIT

Whitebait is a dish, not a fish, and was reportedly invented in the late 1700s by an English fisherman. It consists of very small juvenile fish such as sprats, smelt, and small herring, all dusted in flour and deep-fried. The fish look more like bait for other fish rather than food for people, which may explain the name.

WHITEFISH

Other Names and Species: Bloater, chub, cisco, grayback, inconnu, mountain whitefish, round whitefish

Freshwater

This delicious fish is from the salmon and trout family, but is rarely seen fresh. It comes from the cold lakes of Canada and Alaska, and is usually smoked before reaching our markets. It is high in fat and has white flesh that separates into long flakes. If fresh, the whitefish is excellent grilled, broiled, or poached.

WHITING

See Hake under Cod

CHAPTER 2

Buying and Storing Guide

Buying and Storing Guide

Freshness is the key word in buying fish. Fish begins to deteriorate shortly after it is taken out of the water, so the sooner it is consumed, the better flavor and texture it will have. Everyone knows what a "fishy" smell is, but *fresh* fish does *not* have it. An unpleasant odor is the first clue that fish is getting stale. And it is almost a given that a fishy-smelling fish won't taste very good, either. It won't be terrible, but it won't make fish lovers out of people.

Fish is at its peak the moment it comes from the water, as anyone who has fished for his or her dinner knows. But there are problems that go along with getting the freshest fish.

To begin with, "fresh" fish in the market may already be at least a week old. What has happened over that week is any number of things having to do with the logistics of fishing and distribution. Fishing boats may be out at sea for two days to a week. If the boat stays out a week, a fish caught on the first day will be gutted and iced down very thoroughly in the hold, but it has nonetheless been out of the water for one whole week by the time it reaches the dock.

Since we buy our fish from retail markets rather than directly from fishermen at the docks, the fish must go to a wholesaler who then sells it to the retailers. This process may take one to two whole days. The fish will presumably have been very carefully iced down and will still smell fresh, but again, time has elapsed and flavor has been lost. In addition, this time frame does not account for the importation of fish or for shipping fish from wholesalers to different parts of the country. That may add even more time.

There are positive sides to the story, however. First, many fishing boats are equipped with excellent means of cleaning and icing fish at sea, as well as flash-freezing equipment (a process that freezes fish at a temperature much lower and much more quickly than a standard home freezer). Secondly, some boats do only go out on short trips, and the distribution cycle can be very fast and efficient, bringing fish no more than forty-eight hours old to the market.

Fish from many parts of the world can be flown into U.S. markets, kept fresh by refrigerated transport, thus bringing us fish we would never otherwise be able to taste (unless we went, say, to New Zealand to enjoy their pipi clams or orange roughy). The same is true for midwesterners, who can now have fresh swordfish and mussels from California flown into their markets and restaurants. And as long as we continue to demand freshness from our fishmongers, they will have to pass the message along to their distributors and thus to the fishermen. So don't buy questionable fish, and do complain if the fish you buy isn't top-notch.

JUDGING THE MARKET

Your nose is the best judge of the fish market. The market should have a fresh smell, reminiscent of the sea—not a fishy odor. If it does have a fishy smell, it may not be because of the fish itself, but inadequate cleaning. Even the wholesale fish markets, where huge volumes of fish are cleaned, scaled, and cut up every day, smell of nothing but seaweed and ocean.

The market should be clean and the fish displayed in an orderly fashion. Fish should be kept directly on top of flaked ice, preferably behind a refrigerated glass counter, and whole fish and all cuts should be visible. Metal trays sitting on the ice is a common way of displaying the fish—this is adequate, but the fish should not be sitting in a pool of liquid, and again the cuts should be visible. Prepacked fish *can't* give off an odor through the plastic, so you won't know what you're getting. Be wary of markets that sell fish already packaged.

Markets dedicated to freshness will only sell fish that is in season, or fish they know is flown in fresh. The fishmonger and clerks will be well instructed and should be able to tell you anything you need to know about the fish.

Look for uncomplicated labeling, and familiar names for fish. If the name of a particular fish is unrecognizable, ask what it is. There is not a strict labeling code in the marketing of fish, and sometimes fish markets will embellish the name. But the fish may also be a new variety, so it's best to check. Look for signs marking the fish as "fresh" or "fresh-frozen." "Fresh" should mean the fish has never been frozen, and "fresh-frozen" hopefully means it has been flash-frozen. Unlabeled fish may have been frozen and thawed.

The Fishmonger

Look for a fishmonger you can trust. He or she is the person who should be able to tell you the most important facts about the fish: where it came from, exactly what type of fish it is, when it was caught, and when it came into the shop. A conscientious fishmonger will have found this out before buying from the wholesaler, since it is crucial to the reputation of his or her market.

FISH IN THE MARKET

The ideal way to buy fish is to buy it whole and have the fishmonger cut it up for you while you wait. You can then take the cuts home for dinner, make stock with the bones, and make delicious fish stew the next day with both the stock and the extra meat. But this is not always practical, so it's good to be familiar with the options.

Fish can be divided into three very general categories based on their physical characteristics: **Shellfish** include mollusks and crustaceans such as clams, oysters, shrimp, and lobster. Shellfish is usually sold whole.
Round fish have an oval or circular body, and include salmon, tuna, trout, and bluefish.
Flatfish are flat and broad. Halibut, sole, and flounder are flatfish.

Market Cuts

The market cuts available are basically the same for both round fish and flatfish. They are as follows:
Whole: Also *round*. Fish fresh out of the water is whole fish, ungutted and unscaled. When fish is whole, it is easiest to judge freshness, since the skin and eyes are visible and the scales attached. Ungutted fish deteriorates quickly, however, so whole fish should be dressed as soon as possible.
Dressed: Also *drawn*. The viscera are removed, and the gills may also have been removed. Many fish are dressed at sea and held on ice to slow deterioration. The head and scales are intact, thus the eyes are visible to determine freshness.
Pan-dressed: The viscera and gills are removed, the fish is scaled, the fins and tail are trimmed, and the head may be removed. Smaller fish, such as trout, may be pan-dressed with the head left intact.
Split: A pan-dressed fish opened flat like a book, with the bones left in. The head and tail may be still attached. The skin is left on to keep the flesh intact.
Butterflied: A boned split fish.
Chunk: Also *block, roast*. A section of a large fish, often the tail section, usually including skin and always including bone.
Steaks: Cross-section slices of large dressed fish, usually round fish but sometimes the larger flatfish as well. The backbone is generally left in. Steaks are cut ¾ to 1¾ inches thick. The skin is usually left on to prevent the fish from falling apart when cooking.
Fillets: The sides of the fish, cut and lifted off the backbone and ribs. They are often nearly boneless. The skin may or may not be left on. Quarter-cut fillets are two fillets cut out of one large flatfish fillet.
Butterfly Fillets: Both fillets are removed from either side of the fish but left attached by the skin at the top of the fish along the backbone. These fillets are virtually boneless. The skin is usually left on.
Medallions: A boneless fillet sliced at a very oblique angle into round, flat slices.
Fingers: Finger-length strips, about ¾ inches wide, cut from boneless fillets.
Cubes: Three-quarter-inch cubes cut from boneless fillets or steaks.

BUYING THE FISH

When shopping for fish, the object is to buy the freshest whole or cut fish available. This may mean selecting a different type of fish than you'd planned once you see what is available, so it is important to remain flexible. The best way to get fresh cuts is to select the freshest whole fish and have the fishmonger cut it up. This is also generally more economical, and there are fairly straightforward ways of judging the freshness of whole fish. There are also ways, however, of judging the freshness of cuts. Most types of shellfish are either alive or cooked before you buy them, but again there are guidelines to picking out the best of the bunch. In all fish buying, the three senses you will need to draw on for judging freshness are *smell, sight,* and *feel*.

Selecting Whole Fish

Fresh whole fish will have no "fishy" odor, except for a mild, pleasant smell of the sea or seaweed. (The exceptions are shark and skate, which, because of their metabolic system, will have a slight ammonia odor that is actually an indication of freshness.)

The eyes of a whole fish should be clear and slightly bulging. Cloudy eyes indicate that the fish has been out of the water too long. (The exceptions are red snapper, which has bright red eyes, and some bottom-feeders, such as catfish, which have naturally cloudy eyes.)

The gills will be bright or deep red. Fish with pinkish or dark reddish-brown gills should be avoided.

The skin should be intact, moist, and shiny, and the scales should be attached, not flaking or dry. The skin should not, however, be slimy.

Whole fish will be stiff, not floppy. Press the flesh with your finger. It should feel firm and resilient and leave no indentation.

Selecting Cuts of Fish

Cuts of fish should have no odor (except shark or skate; see above).

The color should be the true color of the fish when raw (i.e., salmon will be bright reddish-orange, sole will be white, red snapper slightly tinged with red, mackerel brownish-gray, etc.). Cuts should be moist and glistening, with no bruises or dark spots, dried-out edges, or browning. If the fish looks watery or unnaturally grayish, it has been improperly frozen and should be avoided.

When you press the flesh with your finger, no indentation should be left in the fish. It should be firm and resilient, not mushy.

Selecting Shellfish

Shellfish must be either alive or cooked, except shrimp, squid, octopus, and soft-shell crab.
Crustaceans include crab, crayfish, lobster, and shrimp.

Live crab, crayfish, and lobster should be very

lively in their tanks. No claws should be missing (unless you are economizing, since one- and no-clawed lobsters and crabs cost less). The shell should be hard.

Raw shrimp, which is not sold live, will be gray in color and moist-looking. The shell and head should be well attached and not dried-out. A slight ammonia odor is an indication that shrimp is stale.

Cooked crustaceans should be firm to the touch and have their tail (and claws, if any) curled in tightly toward their body. The tail will snap back into the curled position when extended and released.

Mollusks include the univalves (one-shelled mollusks): abalone, conch, periwinkle, and whelk; and the bivalves (double-shelled mollusks): clams, mussels, oysters, and scallops. With the exception of scallops, all mollusks should be purchased live when in the shell.

Select mollusks with tightly closed unbroken shells. They should feel heavy but not too much so. If the shell is too light the mollusk may be dead, and if too heavy, full of sand.

Scallops should be cream-colored or ivory, not grayish. They should have slightly rounded and smooth edges, not a "stamped-out" appearance.

Clams and oysters shucked and sold in jars should be plump, and their liquor clear.

Octopus and squid should be sweet-smelling, not grayish or dry-looking.

Selecting Frozen Fish

Frozen fish is difficult to judge because you can't smell it, feel it, or, as is often the case, even see it. But that doesn't necessarily mean it should be avoided.

If the fish or package *does* have any unpleasant odor, don't buy it.

Ideally, buy frozen fish the day before you plan to use it. Pick it up last in the market, and don't let it sit in a hot car or partially thaw. If you do buy it to store, avoid keeping frozen fish for too long. No home freezer can keep fish frozen as solidly as a commercial freezer, and it will soon begin to deteriorate in your own freezer (see ahead to the section on storing fish).

If the fish is marked "flash-frozen"–a technique that freezes it almost instantly at a very low temperature–consider this a plus. If you can see the fish through the wrapper, it should have no discolorations or bruises. Avoid flesh that looks cottony, or has a lot of ice crystals attached to it. Fish frozen in an ice block is acceptable, though. Well-frozen fish should feel as hard as a rock.

The package should be intact, with no holes or rips. Look for dates on the packages and select ones with the most recent mark. The packages underneath the top layer in a market freezer will be frozen more solidly, so don't hesitate to be selective.

DOING YOUR OWN CUTTING UP

The most economical way of buying fish is to buy it whole and have the fishmonger cut it up or cut it up yourself. Judging the freshness of a whole fish is much easier than judging fillets or steaks. In addition, the bones and head can be made into delicious fish stock in less than 45 minutes. The stock can then be frozen for later use in soups and sauces. If you catch your own fish it is important to know how to dress, or fillet it. And if you like the job of preparing whole store bought fish or find you have a whole fish you'd rather cut up, the skills are very handy.

Equipment

Specialized equipment for cleaning and cutting up fish is optional, but it does make the process much easier and less frustrating.

Scaler: Any time the fish is to be served with the skin on, scaling is essential. A fish scaler is a sturdy curved tool with serrated edges for scraping off scales.

Shears: Heavy kitchen or fish shears simplify the jobs of cutting off fins and tails, cutting out gills, eviscerating the fish, and removing the head. They make these jobs safer as well.

Fish Knife: An all-purpose double-edged knife with one sharp edge for cutting and steaking, and a serrated edge for scaling.

Heavy Fish Knife: These heavy-duty knives can have blades up to 20 inches long. The serrated edge can be used for sawing through the thickest backbone or scaling large fish. The blade is also strong enough to be struck with a mallet to go through heavy backbones.

Fillet Knife: A knife with a thin flexible blade 7 to 9 inches long. The filleting knife has a very sharp tip for slicing through the skin of a fish, and is light-weight and maneuverable. Sharpness is crucial. The filleting knife should never be used for cutting through bones.

Carving or Long Filleting Knife: A long, flexible knife that can be used for cutting fillets from very large fish.

Cleaver: Useful for cutting through heavy backbones when steaking fish.

Mallet: Either wooden or rubber, a mallet is used in conjunction with a heavy knife or cleaver for cutting through heads or backbones. Use a wooden mallet for pounding tough shellfish (abalone, conch, octopus, squid steaks, and geoduck) to tenderize.

Tweezers: Heavy-duty tweezers are useful for pulling small bones out of fillets without damaging the meat. Needlenose pliers can also be used.

Cutting Board: A good surface for scaling, filleting, steaking, and boning is a sturdy plastic cutting board that can be sterilized after use and won't hold odors.

Cleaning the Fish

Some basic preparation for whole fish is necessary before butterflying, filleting, or steaking fish. These are the various options for dressing whole fish.

Removing Fins and Tail

With shears or a heavy knife, cut off all fins just behind the bone that connects them to the fish, or as close to the bone as possible. Trim the tail. It is a good idea to trim fins even if you are cutting fillets, since they can sometimes be sharp.

Scaling Fish

Any fish with scales that is to be prepared and served with the skin on must be scaled. Hold the fish by the tail. With a fish scaler, fish knife, or the blunt side of a small knife, scrape the scales off *toward* the head, *against* the direction in which they grow. This job can be done outside to minimize the mess of flying scales, or in a sink of water. Rinse the fish well after scaling, and feel the skin for any scales you have missed.

Eviscerating Fish

After scaling the fish, its entrails must be removed, unless the fishmonger has already done this. The procedure is the same for both flatfish and round fish. With shears or the sharp tip of a knife, make a shallow cut from the vent near the anal fin up to the chinbone of the fish. On flatfish do this with the belly side of the fish facing up. Do not puncture the viscera. Remove the viscera by hooking them with your finger just under the chin and pulling down. Puncture the membrane attached to the ribs and scrape out the remaining matter. Rinse the fish well under gently running water.

Removing the Gills

If you are cooking a whole fish with the head left on, the gills must be removed. Lift the gill covers. With a sharp knife or shears, cut the gills away from the head and pull them out. Rinse the cavity. If you are eviscerating the fish through the gill covers, cut the gills away from the head and pull the gills out with the viscera attached. Reach into the fish through the gill covers and scrape out any remaining matter. Rinse the fish. This leaves the belly skin intact.

Removing the Head

If you are cooking a whole fish with the head off, it is unnecessary to remove the gills. With a heavy knife or cleaver, cut off the head at an angle behind the gill covers from the top of the head to the pelvic fin.

Cutting Up Fish

Pan-Dressing

1. Trim the fins and tail.
2. Scale the fish.
3. Eviscerate the fish.
4. If cooking with the fish head on, remove the gills. If cooking with the fish head off, remove the head.

Splitting

1. Trim the fins and tail.
2. Scale the fish.
3. Eviscerate the fish.
4. If cooking with the fish head on, remove the gills. If cooking with the fish head off, remove the head.
5. Place the fish backbone down and belly up, and open it out.
6. With a heavy knife, cut along one side of the backbone through the rib bones, but *do not sever the skin*.
7. Open the fish out flat. Split fish are cooked with the bones in.

Butterflying

1. Trim the fins and tail.
2. Scale the fish.
3. Eviscerate the fish.
4. If cooking with the fish head on, remove the gills. If cooking with the fish head off, remove the head.
5. Open the fish up and place it flat, flesh side down, on a board. Press gently but firmly on the backbone of the fish to loosen it.
6. Turn the fish over. Beginning at the head, slide a filleting knife under the backbone and perpendicular to it. Loosen and cut the backbone and rib bones away from the flesh, lifting the skeletal structure up as you go, cutting from the head to the tail.
7. Check the flesh for any remaining bones.

Steaking

1. Trim the fins and tail.
2. Scale the fish.
3. Eviscerate the fish.
4. Place the fish on its side. Make the first cut at an angle just behind the gill covers. With a heavy knife, mark off cross-section steaks from ¾ inch to 1½ inches thick, cutting down to the backbone.
5. Slice on down through each steak, cutting through the backbone and using a mallet with the knife if necessary.

Filleting

1. Trim the fins and tail.
2. Eviscerate the fish.
3. Fillet the dark top side of a flatfish first (but either side of a round fish). Place the fish flat on a board with the backbone toward you and the head on the side you cut with. Make a diagonal cut behind the gill covers from the top of the head to the pelvic fin, and all the way down to the bone.
4. Make a shallow, flat cut along the backbone from the head to the tail.
5. Beginning at the top corner (near the head and backbone) of the fish, make a series of sweeping cuts at a slight angle to the backbone and with the knife

almost flat to the rib bones. Continue making these cuts, lifting the fillet up as you go and keeping the knife very flat to the ribs, from the top of the head to the anal fin. Sever the skin.

6. Turn the fish over, leaving the fillet under the fish for support. Repeat steps 3, 4, and 5 on the other side of the fish. Remove both fillets.

7. Feel the flesh for bones, and remove them with tweezers.

Skinning Fillets

1. Place the fillet skin side down on a board.

2. At the tail end, cut through the flesh, angling toward the head end. Holding the flap of tail skin, slide the knife under the flesh along the skin with the knife almost flat. Don't cut through the skin.

Cutting Quarter-cut Fillets

Flatfish fillets can be cut into two pieces along a natural line down the middle of the fillet.

Shellfish

See individual listings for shellfish in Chapter 1, "A Fish Glossary," for information on cleaning and cutting up shellfish.

KEEPING FISH FRESH

Once you have carefully selected the freshest fish in the market, it is important to keep it that way once you get it home, even if you are cooking it within a few hours.

Refrigeration

Any whole fish you plan on storing longer than a few hours should be eviscerated before putting it in the refrigerator. Ice it down if possible, and store it loosely covered for no more than 2 days. Don't allow it to sit in the melted ice.

Store fish cuts in the refrigerator ideally no longer than 24 hours. The fish should be unwrapped, rinsed and patted dry, and rewrapped loosely in butcher or waxed paper and stored in the fridge.

Freezing

Most home freezers are inadequate for properly freezing fish. They simply aren't cold enough. The result is that fish loses moisture and the texture begins to soften, with not very tasty results. In addition, many fish have been frozen or partially frozen on the boat or in transit, and these should not be refrozen. Do not freeze fish that still has gills or has not been eviscerated.

If you are freezing fresh fish, place it in plastic or other airtight wrap and wrap it so that there is as little air as possible in the package. Mark the date and what type of fish it is on the package.

Store lean fish for no more than 2 months, and fatty fish for no more than 1 month.

If you have bought frozen fish, mark it with the date, place it immediately in the freezer, and keep it no longer than 3 months.

Thawing

Thaw frozen fish in the refrigerator unwrapped, placed on several layers of paper towels, and loosely covered. Most fish will thaw in approximately 12 hours, depending on the thickness. Use the fish immediately, preferably just before it is completely thawed.

Shellfish

Shellfish may be stored in the refrigerator, but never immersed in water.

Store clams, crab, crayfish, lobster, mussels, and shrimp in a loose paper bag in the fridge so they can breathe. Keep them no longer than 1 day, and if they die while being stored, discard them. Lobsters, crabs, and crayfish will become sluggish in the fridge, but should show some signs of life.

Oysters should be stored cup side down and loosely covered in the refrigerator for no more than 2 days.

Commercially frozen shellfish will keep up to 2 months in the freezer. Thaw slowly in the refrigerator.

HOW MUCH FISH?

The following is a general guideline for buying *one serving* of fish or shellfish. The fishmonger can also offer advice on how much to buy.

Fish	Per Serving
Whole	¾ to 1 pound
Dressed	¾ pound
Pan-dressed	½ to ¾ pound
Butterflied (boned)	½ pound
Chunk	½ pound
Steaks (bone in)	½ pound
Fillets and steaks (boned)	⅓ to ½ pound

Shellfish	
Clams, average hard-shell	6 to 10
Clams, steamers	12 to 15
Crab, live	2 blues, 1 Dungeness
Crab, lump meat	¼ to ⅓ pound
Crab, soft-shell, average size	2 to 3
Crayfish	8 to 12
Lobster, live	1 to 1½ pounds
Lobster, tails	1 pound
Lobster, lump meat	¼ to ⅓ pound
Mussels, live	8 to 12
Oysters, live	6 to 8
Scallops, bay	12 to 15 (¼ to ⅓ pound)
Scallops, sea	5 to 8 (¼ to ⅓ pound)
Shrimp, jumbo and large	4 to 6
Shrimp, medium	8 to 10
Shrimp, small and tiny	10 to 25
Squid, small 6 inch	4 to 6
Squid, large, steaks	¼ to ⅓ pound

A Word About Nutrition and Safety

Fish is a good bet nutritionally. We should all eat a good deal more of it, because it is better for us in all ways than meat.

Protein

Fish is higher in protein than beef. The average amount of protein in fish is about 19 percent, while most beef contains under 15 percent protein.

Fat

Fish on the average is extremely low in fat. Lean fish is under 5 percent fat, while the fattiest fish is 18 percent. Beef, on the other hand, contains an average of 30 percent fat.

The type of fat in fish is also important, since it contains unsaturated and polyunsaturated fat, as opposed to saturated animal fat. Unsaturated and polyunsaturated fats don't contribute to cholesterol, and some researchers argue that polyunsaturated fish oil actually *reduces* cholesterol. At the very least, fish oil doesn't increase your cholesterol level, and if you are eating low-cholesterol foods, presumably they are replacing other high-cholesterol foods.

Carbohydrates and Calories

Fish contains no carbohydrates to speak of. Because of the low fat content and absence of carbohydrates, fish is very low in calories.

Vitamins and Minerals

Most fish have excellent diets, and we all know that things from the sea are extremely nutritious. Fish is high in vitamins, particularly A and D, and is also high in minerals. It is low, contrary to what one might expect, in sodium. In fact, it is lower in sodium than beef.

Digestibility

Fish has very little connective tissue, which is one reason it cooks so quickly and why it falls apart or "flakes" when cooked, and why it is so highly digestible.

Red Tide

One hazard in eating shellfish is the "red tide," the occurrence of a one-celled organism that renders some shellfish toxic. This organism, called a *dyno-flagellate,* blooms in the summer months, and the clams, mussels, and oysters that live in the wild feed on it. It accumulates in shellfish, creating the build-up of a substance toxic to humans. The toxin may give you "shellfish poisoning"—severe headache, dizziness, stomach upset, or shortness of breath—and can, in extreme cases, be fatal. There is no way to detect this toxin before eating shellfish, and it is not killed when the shellfish is cooked. The only way to avoid it is *not* to eat shellfish during the months of May, June, July, and August, and, to be absolutely sure, September (the usual rule of thumb is to avoid the months without an "r" in the name).

CHAPTER 3

Cooking Tools
and Methods

The secret to cooking fish is to *not overcook it.* Fish almost invariably becomes rather dull-tasting and dry when overcooked. And if it doesn't fall into the dull and dry category when overcooked, it falls into the tough and rubbery category.

Remove the fish from the heat when it is *just* done. If you will be keeping it warm on a platter or in the oven, remove it just seconds *before* it is done (see Judging Doneness, below).

Take the fish out of the refrigerator 20 minutes before cooking. This brings it to room temperature, and allows it to cook more evenly. Ice-cold fish tends to overcook on the outside before it's done on the inside.

Cook fish following the "Canadian Method," created by the Canadian Fish Council. They recommend 10 minutes of total cooking time per 1 inch of thickness measured at the thickest point. This means that a ½-inch fillet cooks in 5 minutes, while a 1½-inch steak cooks in 15. This method is a guideline only, but it comes very close in most cases.

Don't turn thin fillets. Most thin cuts won't have to be turned, even when broiling or grilling.

Leave the bones in when possible. The bones help hold in natural moisture, and make the cooked fish more tender and succulent.

On large whole fish, make four or five ¼-inch-deep slashes on both sides to help the inside cook more evenly.

Fatty or oily fish, such as mackerel, tuna, sablefish, or butterfish, are best cooked using a "dry-heat" cooking method: broiling, baking, or grilling. "Moist-heat" cooking—sautéing, poaching, frying, or steaming—is best for lean fish such as haddock, halibut, and flounder.

Use only nonreactive pans to cook fish. These are lined or made of stainless steel, porcelain enamel, coated or anodyzed aluminum, tin, or glass.

Judging Doneness

Fish is usually translucent in the raw state. Cooked fish loses that translucency and becomes white and opaque.

Most fish separates naturally into flakes when cooked. When the flakes just come apart when prodded, the fish is done.

Use two forks, a skewer or two, or a knife to separate the flakes. When the very center has just a trace of translucency left, remove the fish. The little bit in the center will finish cooking off the heat.

Press gently on the flesh. A cooked fish will feel firm but *not* rock hard to the touch.

POACHING

Poaching means to cook in a simmering liquid. Fish should be completely immersed in a poaching liquid that is kept at such a low simmer as to be almost a mere shudder. Anything more violent may break up the fish and cause it to lose flavor.

The poaching liquids most commonly used are water, wine, fish stock, milk, beer, or juice. Herbs, pepper, vegetables, or spices may also be added to enhance the flavor of the poaching liquid. (See Chapter 4, "Stocks, Sauces, and Relishes," for poaching liquids.)

Large nonreactive skillets are excellent for poaching, as is, of course, a fish poacher. Poach directly on top of the stove or in a very hot oven. Heat-proof glass dishes may also be used for oven poaching.

Cover the fish with the pan lid, a piece of foil, parchment paper, or a lettuce or spinach leaf. The object is to hold in moisture when poaching. Large whole fish may be wrapped in cheesecloth to keep the fish intact. Leave the ends of the cheesecloth long for lifting the cooked fish from the pan. Remove the cloth before storing the fish.

Allow poached whole fish that will be eaten cold to cool in the poaching liquid. Turn off the heat 7 to 10 minutes before the fish is done (the center of the fish will still show some translucency) and leave it covered until completely cool.

Stovetop Poaching

Place the fish in a nonreactive pan large enough to let the fish lie flat. Add enough liquid so that it just covers the fish. Remove the fish and set it aside.

Bring the liquid to a boil. Reduce the heat to very low and carefully lower the fish back into the pan.

Cover the fish and cook it without boiling until the flesh has just lost its translucency.

Large dishes and poaching pans can be straddled across two burners.

Oven Poaching

Preheat the oven to 450°.

Place the fish in a nonreactive pan or dish large enough so that the fish lies flat. Add enough heated poaching liquid to just cover the fish. Cover the pan.

Place the pan in the preheated oven and cook until the flesh has just lost its translucency.

Poaching Tools

Fish Poacher: These are particulary suited to larger fish that will not fit in an ordinary skillet or dish. Generally long narrow oval-shaped pans, they have a

rack for lowering the fish into and lifting it out of the poaching liquid. Diamond-shaped poachers are designed for turbot, but are suitable for most flatfish. Poachers should be made of nonreactive metals such as tin or stainless steel, and should have lids.

Baking Dishes: Some dishes are specifically designed for fish. These are usually oval, and are most often made of earthenware or porcelain. Ovenproof glass baking dishes are also very useful for poaching.

Skillets: Use large skillets for poaching smaller fish and cuts. The fish should always lie flat in the pan. Use nonreactive metals.

BAKING

Baking is a dry-heat method of cooking in which little or no liquid is used. It may also be called roasting. The fish cooks either covered or uncovered, though when covered more moisture will be retained.

Bake whole fish at 375° and smaller fish, steaks, and fillets at a higher temperature, around 425°. The higher heat cooks thin fish and cuts quickly and evenly, while for larger fish a higher temperature would overcook the outside before the inside was done. Large whole fish should be slashed in several places on both sides for more even baking.

Always preheat the oven when baking, so that the fish begins cooking immediately. Fish do not need to be turned during baking, since the heat distribution is even. The Canadian method of cooking fish 10 minutes per inch of thickness is the best timing for baking.

En Papillote

This form of baking is done in a sealed packet. The packet is usually made of parchment paper, but aluminum foil may be used. The fish steams inside the sealed packet, thus retaining moisture and flavor.

Preheat the oven to 375°. Using a piece of parchment paper several inches longer than the fish, fold it in half lengthwise and cut out a large half heart. Open up the paper (you should have a whole heart), butter one side and place the fish on that side. Sprinkle the fish with water or wine, salt and pepper, and a dot of butter. Fold the other half of the heart over the fish. Beginning at the top of the heart, fold the edges over each other, making small secure pleats. At the bottom point of the heart, fold the tip under twice to seal it. A properly sealed packet will puff up and cook the fish evenly.

Place the packet on a baking sheet and bake in the *preheated* oven for approximately 10 minutes for 1-inch-thick fillets. Serve the packets on large plates and let each diner open his or her own.

Oven Frying

This is a way to cook fish that has been dipped in batter. Preheat the oven to 425°. Dip the fish in beaten egg with milk, then into bread crumbs. Arrange on a baking sheet, dab gently with melted butter, and bake uncovered in the *preheated* oven for 5 to 7 minutes for ½-inch thick fillets.

Baking Tools

Covered Dishes: Clay baking dishes or oven-proof glass baking dishes with tops are excellent for baking fish. Soak clay bakers in water for 15 minutes before baking. Any open baking dish may be covered with aluminum foil in lieu of a lid.

Parchment: This heavy baking paper is found in specialty cookware stores. It comes on a roll or in flat folded sheets.

Open Dishes: Fish can be baked on baking sheets, in open casseroles, or in baking pans. Avoid aluminum pans.

BROILING

Broiling is a dry-heat method of cooking in which the heat comes from one source: an overhead gas or electric broiling element in your oven. Broil fish 1½ to 4 inches from the heat source.

Broiling is ideal for fatty fish such as mackerel, tuna, salmon, and butterfish. Cook these fairly close to the heat. Leaner fish is also excellent broiled, but benefits from a basting sauce or marinade and a bit more distance from the heat.

The broiler should be preheated, but always remove the broiler pan first. A hot broiler pan will cook the underside of the fish too quickly.

Fillets under ¾-inch thick do not need to be turned. Fragile fish is best left unturned as well.

Use the Canadian method of cooking fish for 10 minutes per inch of thickness for timing broiled fish. Whole fish should be slashed several times on both sides for even cooking.

Broiling Tools

Long-bladed Spatula: A spatula with an extra-long blade and a crooked handle is ideal for turning pieces of fish in the broiler. Use an extra spatula to help the fish onto the spatula used for turning.

Broiler Pans: Most oven broilers are equipped with pans that fit into slots at several distances from the heat source.

Baking Sheets: Baking sheets are good substitutes for broiler pans.

Shallow Casseroles: Shallow ovenproof casseroles can be used on top of or in place of broiler pans.

GRILLING

Grilling is a dry-heat method of cooking. It brings out the full flavor of the fish, which the smoky charcoal enhances. Fish cooks quickly on the grill, and remains very tender and succulent.

Both lean and fatty fish cook well on the grill, though leaner fish benefit from a half-hour marinade or a basting sauce. It is always best to brush any fish with a little oil before grilling to keep it from sticking to the grills.

Allow the coals to burn down to a light coating of gray ash over red-hot coals, which takes about 40 minutes. Don't begin cooking while the coals are still

black and flaming. The fire is right when you are able to hold your hand 6 inches above the coals for about 6 seconds.

Preheat the grill rack and oil it. This both sears the fish and keeps it from sticking to the hot bars. The ideal position for the grill rack above the fire is about 6 inches. Place fish on the grill rack perpendicular to the bars. Turn the fish only once if necessary, and avoiding moving it any more than that.

Fragile fish can be cooked on a sheet of oiled perforated aluminum foil. Be sure to make plenty of holes in the foil so that the grill smoke can penetrate and flavor the fish.

Fish will cook on a covered or uncovered grill, though whole fish should be slashed several times on both sides and grilled covered. Thin fillets need not be turned, particulary if the grill is covered. Use the Canadian method of 10 minutes per inch of thickness for timing.

Grill Tools

Grills: Grills come in all sizes and shapes, and are built for charcoal, gas, or electricity. Charcoal grills may be messy, but gas and electric grills simply don't provide the distinctive charcoal flavor. You can put charcoal pieces or aromatic wood chips in some gas and electric grills, however, which adds flavorful smoke. Check the manufacturer's instructions to be certain.

Charcoal: We recommend mesquite or hardwood charcoal. It is pure (no fillers or starters added), and burns hotter and cleaner. It can also be reused. Use kindling, a cylindrical chimney, or an electric starter to light coals. We do not recommend fluid or solid fire starters, as they add a chemical taste to the delicate flavor of fish.

Hinged Grills: These grilling "baskets" come in many sizes and shapes. They are fish-shaped, round, square, or rectangular, with two thin wire racks hinged at the side to hold the food between them. The grills must be oiled first, and can be lined with branches of fresh herbs such as rosemary, thyme, or oregano, or grape leaves, lettuce, spinach, or fennel branches. Nestle the hinged grill directly on the coals or on top of the grills. The hinged grill makes it easy to turn the fish: simply turn the whole thing over.

Long-bladed Spatula: A long-bladed spatula with a crooked handle makes turning long fillets or whole fish possible without breaking them up. Use another spatula to help move the fish onto the spatula used for turning.

Long-handled Tongs: Long-handled spring-loaded tongs are perfect for turning small pieces of fish and shellfish.

Long-handled Basting Brushes: Use these for basting fish on the grill, since the long handle keeps your hands away from sudden flare-ups that might be caused by the oil.

PAN-FRYING, SAUTÉING, AND STIR-FRYING

These three moist-heat cooking methods are very similar, with the difference mainly in the cooking temperature.

Pan-frying

Pan-frying is excellent for cooking small whole fish less than 10 inches long. The fish is cooked quickly so that little moisture is lost, and uncovered so that the skin of the fish becomes crispy, not soggy or steamed. Dust fish lightly with flour before pan-frying to seal in moisture, but use no more of a batter than that.

Use medium-low heat for pan-frying. Use oils that don't burn at high temperatures, such as peanut, or safflower, clarified butter, or a combination of clarified butter and oil.

Sautéing

When sautéing fish, toss or shake it in the hot pan to sear and quickly cook it. This method is suited to thin fillets, and though they are too fragile to knock around in the pan, sauté them over higher heat than when pan-frying, with slightly less oil, and shake the pan gently to keep the fish from sticking. Dust the fish very lightly with flour and cook it in hot safflower, peanut, or olive oil, clarified butter, or a combination of butter and oil. Butter burns at too low a temperature to be used alone for sautéing.

Begin sautéing at medium-high heat, to sear the fish. The temperature may then be reduced to finish cooking if the fish is getting too brown. Do not cover the pan.

After the fish is sautéed, a little liquid may be added to the pan to deglaze it. If the fish is still in the pan, this further cooks the fish and flavors it, and is a form of *braising*.

Stir-Frying

Stir-frying is another form of sautéing, but uses higher heat, and a wok instead of a skillet or sauté pan. In stir-frying, the fish is typically sliced into bite-sized pieces and tossed about very quickly in hot peanut or safflower oil, sometimes with a drop or two of Asian sesame oil. The food is kept moving constantly while it cooks. Soy sauce, vinegar, or rice wine may be added at the end to moisten the fish, or a flavored cornstarch, water, and soy mixture can be added to create a thicker sauce.

Pan-frying, Sautéing, and Stir-frying Tools

Skillets and Sauté Pans: Slope-sided skillets or straight-sided sauté pans are best for pan-frying and sautéing. If pan-frying whole fish, use a pan that is at least as large as the fish. Nonreactive pans of stainless steel, tin-lining, porcelain enamel, or anodyzed aluminum are best.

Wok: A bowl-shaped wok of thin metal can be placed directly on the flame of a gas burner. Flat-bottomed woks are made for electric burners, but their shape makes them more like a skillet than a wok. Electric woks won't reach the temperatures that a bowl-shaped wok on a gas flame will, and are therefore less effective. A wok ring balances the wok on a gas burner and makes stir-frying easier.

Spring-loaded Tongs: These are useful for turning small pieces of fish while pan-frying.

Long-bladed Spatula: With the long blade you can turn large pieces of fish without breaking them up.

DEEP-FRYING AND SHALLOW-FRYING

In both deep-frying and shallow-frying the fish is first coated with a batter, and then fried in very hot oil. When deep-frying, however, the fish is completely immersed in oil, while in shallow-frying the fish is cooked in an inch or less of oil and must be turned. Frying is a very traditional way of cooking fish, from the fish and chips of England to deep-fried catfish and hush puppies from the American South. The batter crisps quickly in the oil, forming a shell that keeps the oil from penetrating the fish. The fish inside the batter casing is light and moist, but not greasy.

The secret to good frying is the oil. Not only the type, but the temperature is important. Oils that don't burn at high temperatures are required, such as peanut, safflower, corn, or vegetable.

The oil must be preheated to between 350° and 375°, and kept at that temperature as closely as possible. Oil that isn't hot enough will make a batter coating soggy. To test oil without a thermometer or electric skillet or fryer, drop a small cube of bread into it when you think it is hot. The bread should brown and crisp in less than 1 minute.

Keep both the batter and the fish cold until just before cooking. The batter is less likely to absorb as much oil when cold. Dry the fish before dipping it into the batter. Once the fish is covered with batter, avoid rubbing off any batter with your fingers.

Lower the fish *carefully* into the hot oil, and allow the oil to reheat to 375° before adding more fish. For best results, don't crowd the pan. Don't cover the fryer or pan as that will cause a soggy coating.

If the oil smokes, it may be beginning to burn. Allow the oil to cool a bit before adding more fish. There may also be bits of batter that are burning, which should be removed with a slotted spoon.

Frying oil can be reused several times. Fry a potato slice after everything else is cooked to clear the oil. Allow the oil to cool completely, and strain it through cheesecloth into a jar. The oil can be kept in the refrigerator for several months, but should be used for fish only.

Safety Tips

Frying can be tricky business, since it involves a good deal of hot oil. Always have the lid to the fryer or pan near by, in case of a flame-up. Don't move the pan around on the burner, as it could cause a flame-up. Don't use a pan that is too shallow for the amount of oil you need. The pan should be at least one-third deeper than the amount of oil used. Don't allow the flames of the burner to lick up around the sides of the pan. Either turn the heat down or use a larger pan. Keep the pan away from other burners with open flames.

If there is a flame-up, put the lid on and turn off the heat under the pan. That will extinguish the flame. Do not attempt to douse it with water, by all means don't rush the pan over to the sink, and don't use a fire extinguisher unless you know it is effective on grease fires.

Splatter screens for shallow frying are great protection against popping oil. Don't drip any water into the oil, since that will cause it to pop and splatter.

Wear long sleeves and an apron to protect against possible popping or splatter.

When shallow-frying, turn the food carefully, and preferably away from you. Don't juggle food precariously above the hot oil, or it may drop into the hot oil and splash you.

Deep-frying

In a deep-fryer or deep heavy pot, heat at least 3 inches of oil to 375°.

Carefully lower the batter-coated fish into the oil and cook until deep golden brown.

Lift the fish from the oil with a slotted spoon and drain on paper towels.

Shallow-frying

Fill a deep skillet with ¾ to 1 inch of oil. Heat to 375°.

Carefully lower the batter-coated fish into the oil. Cook one side until deep golden brown. Carefully turn the fish, and avoid puncturing the batter casing. Cook that side until golden brown.

Remove and drain on paper towels.

Deep-frying and Shallow-frying Tools

Deep-fryer: Deep-fryers are usually deep pots with two handles and a basket insert, with rests to hold the basket above the hot oil to drain the food.

Deep-frying Basket: Start with the wire baskets in place in the pan, and heat the oil. After the fish is lowered into the oil and cooked, the basket is used for lifting it out and draining it. Baskets have a handle for lifting, and often will have rests for propping the food above the oil to drain.

Electric Deep-fryer: This deep electric pot with a frying basket has a temperature control for maintaining an even frying temperature.

Skillet: Use a large skillet, preferably with straight, deep sides, for shallow-frying. Cast-iron skillets work well, but heat up and cool down slowly.

Electric Skillet: An electric pan with a temperature control for even shallow-frying.

Frying Thermometer: A sure way to maintain an even temperature in a non-electric frying pan is with a specialized frying thermometer.

Wok: A wok can be used with great success for deep-frying, and less oil need be used. Never fill a wok more than half full, as it becomes much too unstable.

Slotted Spoon: A tool for lifting out fried food without removing a spoonful of hot oil is convenient when frying. A tempura spoon is also useful for lifting fried food.

STEAMING

Steaming is the most natural method of moist-heat cooking, and it adds no fat to fish. Fish is steamed above about 1 inch of water, wine, or other liquid to which seasonings and herbs may be added. The steaming pot is covered to create steam all around the fish. The liquid should be kept at a good boil, but not too hard.

Any surface is suitable for steaming on, as long as the fish is surrounded by steam in a pot with a tight-fitting lid. Fish may be steamed on a plate with very good results. Invert two small heatproof glasses in the bottom of the steaming pot and rest the plate on top of them. The plate should be at least 1 inch smaller than the width of the pot to make it easy to get in and out.

Left: Skewers, large and small seafood forks, lobster crackers, molds, a flat grater for steaming, and a long-bladed spatula are all tools for preparing and serving seafood. Below: A sturdy, short-bladed oyster knife is used to pry apart the oyster shell near the hinge. See page 24 for further information on shucking oysters.

Steaming is good for all types of fish. Fatty fish won't need extra oil, and lean fish stays moist. Bivalves such as clams and mussels are best steamed in very little liquid. Other shellfish may be steamed as well.

Steaming Tools

Seafood Cooker: This is a large covered pot, for steaming clams or mussels.

Large Pot: A pot large enough to hold steamers or plates is best.

Wok: Fish can be steamed in a wok with a lids. Place the fish in a bamboo or metal steamer, on a flat hand grater propped up inside the wok, on a plate held up by two crossed chopsticks inside the wok, or directly on parallel chopsticks.

Fish Poacher: The inside rack of a fish steamer can sometimes be inverted or the handles folded under to support the rack for use as a steamer inside the poacher.

Bamboo Steamer: This basket steamer is best used in a wok, where it rests suspended above the liquid. Use it for steaks and fillets, or for shellfish of all types.

Metal Steamer: This fold-out steamer sits a little more than an inch above the steaming liquid. It is stainless steel so it won't react with wine or vinegar, and it has a central post for lifting it out of the pot. This steamer is suitable for small fillets and steaks.

BOILING

Most fish is too fragile to boil, except for lobster, crab, and crayfish, and raw squid when lightly cooking it for salad.

Water, or water combined with beer, wine, or herbs is suitable for boiling seafood. Bring the liquid to a full boil and drop in the live shellfish. Start timing when the water returns to a boil.

Boiling Tools

Stockpot or Lobster Pot: A large covered stockpot or lobster pot, preferably of lightweight enameled aluminum, with at least a 16-quart capacity. Use smaller stockpots for crayfish and squid.

STEWING

Stewing fish generally means to combine it with a liquid, vegetables (usually at least tomatoes), herbs, and other seasonings and simmer it slowly. The flavors are more united in stews than in other quick moist-heat cooking techniques.

Stewing Tools

Stew Pot: A large, heavyweight pot of nonreactive metal. Stew pots should have lids.

Tools for Opening and Serving Shellfish

There are many specialized tools that go along with opening and serving shellfish. Most of them are not essential, but they make the job and the presentation much easier.

Oyster Knife

For opening the complicated oyster shell, an oyster knife is almost a must. An oyster knife has a short, sturdy, pointed blade. The blade may or may not be sharp for severing the muscle from the shell. The handle is often thick at the blade end to serve as a guard, so that when forcing the knife between the shells the guard stops the knife at the shell. Wear a mitt or hold the oyster with a heavy cloth when shucking. (A screwdriver has also been found to serve in a pinch.)

Clam Knife

The tip of the clam knife is blunt, since instead of forcing the tip in, the side of the knife is worked in to pry apart the shells of the clam. Sometimes the two features are combined, however, for an "oyster and clam" knife.

Clam Opener

This scissorlike contraption forces the shells apart, but unfortunately cuts the meat while doing it. Use it if the clam meat is to be chopped, and shuck clams over a bowl to catch the juices.

Shrimp Sheller/Deveiner

Insert this sharp curved tool between the shell and meat of the shrimp at the head end, and run it down to the tail. The pointed end cuts out the vein, and when the tool is lifted off, the shell and vein comes with it. Use it on headless raw or cooked shrimp.

Seafood Forks

These narrow two-pronged forks will reach into all but the most narrow shells.

Nutcrackers and Nutpicks

These are probably the most commonly used tools for cracking lobster and crab and picking the delicious meat out of the shells.

Lobster Crackers

Lobster crackers are the same basic tool as a nutcracker, but are usually shaped like the claws of a lobster.

Lobster Pincers

Another scissorlike tool that both cracks the shell and extracts the meat from the lobster.

Lobster Pick

A long, thin two-pronged pick for extracting the tiniest bits of lobster meat from the shells.

Butter Warmers

These are small bowls suspended on stands over a candle for warming dipping butters.

CHAPTER 4

*Stocks, Sauces,
and Relishes*

Stocks, Sauces, and Relishes

WHITE WINE FISH STOCK
(FUMET BLANC)   Makes 7 cups

Use fish stock as a poaching liquid and in making sauces, soups, stews, chowders, and bisques. It is very easy to make—simply ask your fishmonger to throw in some trimmings for stock when you are buying fish. He may or may not charge you for it, but it won't be much if he does. The stock cooks for 40 minutes at the most, so it can be made the same evening you need it. Fish stock can be frozen, and we suggest freezing it in 1½- to 3-cup quantities.

> 4 pounds fish trimmings (heads and bones)
> 2 cups dry white wine
> 8 cups water
> 1 onion, quartered
> 1 carrot, cut up
> 4 parsley sprigs
> 3 fresh thyme sprigs
> Bay leaf
> 8 peppercorns

Put all the ingredients in a large stockpot.

Cook uncovered over low heat for 30 to 40 minutes. Skim the foam periodically.

Strain the stock through several layers of cheesecloth.

RED WINE FISH STOCK
(FUMET ROUGE)   Makes 7 cups

This is a more intensely flavored stock to use with more assertively flavored fish. Use it also for tomato-based sauces, soups, stews, and chowders.

> 4 pounds fish trimmings (heads and bones)
> 4 cups dry red wine
> 8 cups water
> 1 onion, quartered
> 1 carrot, cut up
> 2 garlic cloves, slightly crushed
> 6 to 8 large mushrooms, halved
> 8 parsley sprigs
> 3 thyme sprigs
> 1 bay leaf
> 8 peppercorns

Put all the ingredients in a large stockpot.

Cook uncovered over low heat for 30 to 40 minutes. Skim the foam periodically.

Strain the broth through several layers of cheesecloth.

COURT BOUILLON

Court bouillon is a broth used primarily for poaching fish. Unlike fish stock, it is made *without* fish bones. Court bouillon has a mild flavor, but once the fish has cooked in it, it becomes a light fish stock that can be reduced for sauces or used in soups.

> 1 cup dry white wine
> ½ onion
> 1 carrot, cut up
> ½ celery stalk, cut up
> 3 parsley sprigs
> 1 fresh thyme sprig, or a pinch of dried thyme
> Bay leaf
> Pinch of salt
> 6 peppercorns

Put fish in a pan to be used for poaching. Add all the ingredients, then add water to just barely cover the fish.

CHAMPAGNE COURT BOUILLON

Champagne court bouillon adds a sweeter, more delicate flavor to poached fish.

> 1 cup champagne
> 1 small carrot, cut up
> 1 small leek, white part only, cut up
> 3 parsley sprigs
> 1 fresh thyme sprig, or a pinch of dried thyme
> Pinch of salt
> 6 white peppercorns

Put fish in a pan to be used for poaching. Add all the ingredients, then add water to just barely cover the fish.

ORANGE COURT BOUILLON

A delicious sauce can be made directly from this court bouillon. Use a firm, mild-tasting white fish.

> ¾ cup freshly squeezed orange juice
> ¼ cup dry white wine
> ½ orange, thinly sliced
> 1 green onion, sliced
> Freshly ground pepper

Put fish in a pan to be used for poaching. Add all the ingredients, then add water to just barely cover the fish.

Orange Cream Sauce: After poaching the fish, remove it to a warm platter. Remove and reserve the orange slices. Pour off all but ⅓ cup of the poaching liquid. Whisk in ½ cup cream and reduce the sauce over medium-high heat for 5 minutes, whisking constantly. Pour the sauce immediately over the fish, and arrange the orange slices on top.

MILK COURT BOUILLON

Milk court bouillon adds only a slight sweetness to poached fish, and no wine flavor. It also keeps fish very white.

> 1 cup milk
> 3 parsley sprigs
> Pinch of salt
> 6 white peppercorns

Put fish in a pan to be used for poaching. Add all the ingredients, then add water to just barely cover the fish.

MAYONNAISE AND VARIATIONS
Makes 1 generous cup

No mayonnaise tastes quite like homemade. It improves the flavor of all the mayonnaise-based sauces, as well. Even the much-maligned tartar sauce is redefined by homemade mayo. Use good-quality oil and vinegar for mayonnaise, because their flavors will shine through. We like peanut or safflower oil, because they are mild and polyunsaturated. Olive oil makes an assertive mayonnaise, depending on the strength of the oil. Try using olive oil when making *aïoli* and Red Pepper Mayonnaise. Mayonnaise can be made in a blender or food processor as well. Follow the instructions for making it by hand, taking care to add the oil very slowly while the machine is running. *Important:* Whether making mayonnaise by hand or in a blender, have all ingredients at room temperature before beginning this easy but sometimes temperamental sauce.

> 2 egg yolks
> 1 heaping teaspoon Dijon mustard
> 1 tablespoon good-quality red or white wine vinegar
>   or fresh lemon juice
> ¼ teaspoon salt
> ⅛ teaspoon freshly ground white pepper
> 1 to 1¼ cups good-quality oil

In a large bowl, whisk all the ingredients except the oil together.

Add the oil in a very fine stream, whisking all the while. As the mayonnaise begins to thicken, increase the flow of oil. If the oil gets ahead of you and the mayonnaise begins to separate, stop the flow of oil and just whisk for a moment until the sauce coalesces. Then resume adding the oil.

When all the oil has been added or the mayonnaise is the desired thickness, adjust the seasonings. Mayonnaise will keep in the refrigerator for 1 to 2 weeks.

Variations:
Aïoli: When making mayonnaise, add 2 to 3 garlic cloves, minced to a paste with a pinch of salt, to the egg yolks before adding the oil. Blend well and follow the remaining steps for making mayonnaise. For a quick *aïoli*, blend 2 to 3 garlic cloves, minced to a paste, into 1 cup prepared mayonnaise.

Aïoli with Lemon and Basil: When making mayonnaise, replace the vinegar with 3 tablespoons of lemon juice and add 2 to 3 garlic cloves, minced to a paste with a pinch of salt, to the egg yolks before adding the oil. Blend well and follow the remaining steps for making mayonnaise. To 1 cup prepared *aïoli*, add 1 tablespoon minced fresh basil or 1 teaspoon dried. For a quick *aïoli* with Lemon and Basil, blend 2 to 3 garlic cloves, minced to a paste, 1 tablespoon lemon juice, and basil into 1 cup prepared mayonnaise.

Avocado: To 1 cup prepared mayonnaise, add 1 well-mashed avocado and 1 teaspoon fresh lemon juice. Season with salt and freshly ground black pepper.

Green: To 1 cup prepared mayonnaise, add plenty of finely minced watercress, parsley, tarragon, chives, or spinach, or any combination of these.

Lemon-Dill: To ½ cup prepared mayonnaise, add 1 tablespoon fresh lemon juice and 1 heaping tablespoon fresh dill or 1 teaspoon dried dill.

Mousseline: When making mayonnaise, reserve the egg whites. Whip the egg whites until soft peaks form, and fold them into the prepared mayonnaise. Mayonnaise mousseline is a fluffier, lighter mayo that has fewer calories per tablespoon.

Red Pepper: To ¼ cup prepared mayonnaise add one-half of a pureed roasted and peeled red pepper. Season with salt and freshly ground black pepper.

Russe: To ½ cup prepared mayonnaise add 1 tablespoon crushed caviar and ½ teaspoon Dijon mustard. Season with freshly ground white pepper.

TARTAR SAUCE NO. 1   Makes 1½ cups

> 1 cup mayonnaise, preferably homemade (see above)
> 2 tablespoons capers, drained
> 4 pitted black olives, chopped
> 1 hard-cooked egg, chopped
> 1 tablespoon chopped fresh parsley
> 1 tablespoon chopped fresh chervil (optional)
> 2 teaspoons fresh lemon juice
> Salt and freshly ground pepper to taste

Mix all the ingredients well, season to taste, and serve.

TARTAR SAUCE NO. 2   Makes 1½ cups

> 1 cup mayonnaise, preferably homemade (see above)
> 4 to 5 small sour pickles (gherkins or *cornichons*),
>   chopped
> 4 green olives with pimientos, chopped
> 1 tablespoon minced onion
> 1 teaspoon Dijon mustard
> 1 tablespoon minced fresh parsley
> 1 teaspoon minced fresh chives
> Salt and freshly ground pepper

Mix all the ingredients well, season to taste, and serve.

REMOULADE   Makes 1 cup

> ¾ cup mayonnaise, preferably homemade (see above)
> 1 garlic clove, minced to a paste
> 1½ teaspoons minced fresh tarragon, or ½ teaspoon
>   dried tarragon
> 2 teaspoons Dijon mustard
> 2 teaspoons minced fresh parsley
> 1 teaspoon minced anchovy or anchovy paste
> Freshly ground pepper

Mix all the ingredients well, add pepper to taste, and serve.

HOLLANDAISE

Makes ¾ cup

Hollandaise is delicious on most white-fleshed fish, particularly milder-flavored fish. When making hollandaise, it is important *never* to let the water boil in the bottom of the double boiler. It should barely simmer, and the top pan should not be touching the water.

3 egg yolks
1 tablespoon fresh lemon juice
1 tablespoon cold water
1 stick unsalted butter, cut into 8 pieces and softened
Salt and freshly ground white pepper

In the top of a double boiler over very low heat, whisk the egg yolks with the lemon juice and water until foamy.

Drop in a piece of butter and whisk until the butter starts to melt and blend with the yolks. Remove the pan from the heat if the sauce begins to cook too fast at any time while cooking, or else it will curdle.

Continue adding butter piece by piece, whisking after each addition until the butter has just melted and been incorporated. The sauce should become thick. Season to taste.

Keep the sauce warm in the double boiler over extremely low heat. If butter separates a bit on the top of the sauce, whisk in a teaspoon or so of cold water to re-emulsify the sauce. If the sauce becomes too thick, whisk in another tablespoon or so of butter.

Sauce Mousseline: To prepared hollandaise, fold in ⅓ cup heavy cream, whipped.

Mustard Hollandaise: To prepared hollandaise, stir in 2 teaspoons Dijon mustard, or any flavored mustard.

BÈARNAISE SAUCE

Makes 1 cup

See the preceding recipe for hollandaise for tips on how to make this wonderful classic sauce.

3 egg yolks
1 tablespoon dry white wine
2 tablespoons white wine vinegar
3 chopped shallots
1 garlic clove, minced
1 tablespoon minced fresh tarragon, or 1 teaspoon dried tarragon
2 teaspoons minced fresh parsley
1 stick unsalted butter, cut into 8 pieces and softened
Salt and freshly ground black pepper

In the top of a double boiler over very low heat, whisk the egg yolks until foamy. Add the wine, vinegar, shallots, garlic, tarragon, and parsley and whisk until well blended.

Drop in a piece of butter and whisk until the butter begins to melt and blend with the yolks. When incorporated, continue adding the butter, piece by piece, whisking after each addition. The sauce should be thick. If at any time the sauce begins to cook too quickly, remove it from the heat or it will begin to curdle.

Salt and pepper to taste. Keep the sauce warm in the top of the double boiler over extremely low heat.

COMPOUND BUTTERS/ BASTING SAUCES

Compound butters are an easy way to flavor fish. Slice off "coins" to melt over hot fish or to flavor sauces, or melt the butters for grilling and broiling basting sauces.

Allow 1 stick (unless otherwise specified) of unsalted butter to soften in a bowl out of the refrigerator until malleable but not melting or oily. With a fork or a small wooden spoon, thoroughly blend in any of the following combinations.

In the middle of a square sheet of waxed paper, parchment paper, or aluminum foil, form the butter into a 6-inch log. Fold the paper over the butter and mold the log into a uniform cylinder, rolling the paper up as you go. Twist the ends.

Firm the butter in the refrigerator. Use immediately or store in the freezer, tightly wrapped, indefinitely. Cut off pats as needed.

Anchovy: To ½ stick of butter, add 1 tablespoon minced anchovy and freshly ground black pepper to taste

Basil: 2 tablespoons chopped fresh basil, salt and freshly ground white pepper to taste

Caper: To ½ stick of butter, add 1 tablespoon crushed drained capers

Caviar: 1 ½ tablespoons caviar, 2 teaspoons minced shallot, freshly ground black pepper to taste

Chive: 2 heaping tablespoons minced fresh chives, salt and freshly ground white pepper to taste

Cilantro/Lime: 2 tablespoons chopped fresh cilantro, 2 teaspoons fresh lime juice, salt and freshly ground white pepper to taste

Coral (Roe): To ½ stick butter, add 1 coral (the roe of a lobster) minced to a paste, salt and freshly ground white pepper to taste

Dill and Lemon: 2 heaping tablespoons chopped fresh dill, juice of ½ lemon, salt and freshly ground white pepper to taste

Garlic: 3 to 4 cloves garlic minced to a paste with a pinch of salt, freshly ground white pepper to taste

Parsley: 2 tablespoons minced fresh parsley, salt and freshly ground white pepper to taste

Pine Nut: ¼ cup pine nuts toasted until light brown in a 375° oven and finely chopped, salt and freshly ground white pepper to taste

Sage: 2 tablespoons minced fresh sage, salt and freshly ground black pepper to taste

Tarragon: 2 tablespoons minced fresh tarragon, salt and freshly ground black pepper to taste

Tomalley: To ½ stick butter, 1 tomalley (the green liver of a lobster), minced to a paste, salt and freshly ground black pepper to taste

BEURRE BLANC
(WHITE WINE BUTTER SAUCE)   Makes ½ cup

This classic sauce should have a soft, creamy, lightly whipped consistency. Make it as close to the last minute as possible, as it does not hold well. Use a stainless steel saucepan or skillet to prevent any reaction with the vinegar. The sauce may be strained before serving to remove the shallots, but we like ours with a little texture. Whisk in any fresh minced herb to flavor the sauce if desired, or try flavored vinegars such as tarragon, basil, or raspberry. The classic, simple flavor of *beurre blanc* is excellent over nearly every fish, prepared any way.

3 shallots, finely chopped
½ cup dry white wine or white wine vinegar
3 tablespoons heavy cream
1 stick cold unsalted butter, cut into 8 pieces
Salt and freshly ground white pepper

Combine the shallots and wine in a small stainless steel saucepan. Over medium heat, reduce the mixture to about 1 tablespoon. Reduce heat to low, add the cream, and reduce by about half.

Over very low heat, whisk in 1 piece of the butter. When it is completely incorporated, and add the next piece. Continue adding butter and whisking after each addition until all the butter is incorporated. The sauce should be quite smooth. Strain out the shallots, if desired.

Season to taste with salt and pepper. Serve immediately.

BEURRE ROUGE
(RED WINE BUTTER SAUCE)   Makes ½ cup

This full-bodied sauce is great with swordfish, shark, and tuna. The red wine vinegar may be replaced by flavored vinegars, or try Madeira, Marsala, or port.

3 shallots, finely chopped
½ cup dry red wine or red wine vinegar
1 stick cold unsalted butter, cut into 8 pieces
Salt and freshly ground pepper

Combine the shallots and wine in a small stainless steel saucepan. Over medium heat, reduce the mixture to about 1 tablespoon.

Over very low heat, whisk in 1 piece of the butter. When it is completely incorporated, and add the next piece. Continue adding butter and whisking after each addition until all the butter is incorporated. The sauce should be quite smooth. Strain out the shallots, if desired.

Season to taste with salt and pepper. Serve immediately.

LEMON BUTTER SAUCE   Makes 1 cup

Capers are a nice addition to this sauce, which goes well with any of the flatfish (sole, flounder, or halibut), or with fish from the cod family.

1 stick unsalted butter
2 tablespoons heavy cream
Juice of 1 lemon
2 teaspoons minced fresh parsley
Salt and freshly ground white pepper to taste

In a small stainless steel saucepan over low heat, melt the butter. Whisk in the cream and heat through. Remove from heat and whisk in the remaining ingredients. Season to taste and serve immediately.

ALMOND BUTTER SAUCE   Makes ½ cup

Delicious with sole.

6 tablespoons unsalted butter
½ cup slivered blanched sliced almonds
1 tablespoon fresh lemon juice
1 teaspoon minced fresh parsley
Salt and freshly ground pepper

In a small stainless steel skillet over medium-low heat, melt the butter. Add the almonds and sauté until light brown, stirring constantly to prevent them from cooking unevenly. When the almonds are brown, remove the pan from the heat. Add the lemon juice, allowing it to foam up and cook down for a moment.

Add the parsley and season to taste with salt and pepper. Serve immediately.

BROWN BUTTER   Makes ½ cup

Brown butter has a slightly nutty flavor, and combined with lemon juice is delicious over sauteed, grilled, or broiled fish.

6 tablespoons unsalted butter
Juice of ½ lemon
1 heaping tablespoon chopped fresh parsley
Salt and freshly ground pepper

In a saucepan over medium heat, cook the butter until it is just brown. Whisk in the lemon juice until well incorporated.

Whisk in the parsley and season to taste. Serve immediately.

RED PEPPER BUTTER SAUCE   Makes 1 cup

This creamy sauce is not only flavorful, combining the smoky taste of roasted pepper with sweet cream, but it is beautiful to look at as well. It is perfect for grilled or broiled fish, particularly swordfish and mahi-mahi.

1 large red bell pepper
6 tablespoons unsalted butter
1 small onion, coarsely chopped
¼ cup heavy cream
Salt and freshly ground black pepper

Roast the red pepper: Under a broiler or over the open flame of a gas burner or grill, blister the skin of the pepper all over (it should be quite thoroughly black). Place the pepper in a paper bag for 15 minutes to cool and steam. Remove the pepper, cut off the stem and seeds, and scrape off all the skin with the blunt side of a knife. Do not rinse the pepper; the few charred bits that may remain will not hurt. Chop the pepper and set aside. You should have about ½ cup.

In a small saucepan, melt the butter and sauté the onion until translucent. Remove from heat and allow to cool a bit.

Put the red pepper, butter, and sauteed onion in a blender or food processor and puree until smooth. Scrape the pureed pepper back into the saucepan.

Add the cream and heat gently. Do not boil. Season to taste with salt and pepper and serve.

CLARIFIED BUTTER

Clarified butter is excellent for sautéing any fish, since the solids that cause butter to burn at low temperatures have been removed. This butter keeps well in the refrigerator in a tightly covered container for up to 3 weeks, and it can also be frozen.

2 sticks (1 cup) unsalted butter, cut into quarters

Place the butter chunks in a small heatproof glass bowl (a 2-cup Pyrex measuring cup works well). Lower the bowl into a saucepan with 1 inch of water simmering in the bottom.

When the butter has melted, remove it from the heat. Allow it to cool for 15 minutes.

Spoon the milky white solids off the top. (They can be discarded or used over hot fish, meat, or vegetables in place of regular butter.) Carefully pour off the clarified butter, leaving the watery substance at the bottom, or spoon the clarified butter into a container.

CRÈME FRAÎCHE   Makes 1 cup

In France, *crème fraîche* is the result of the ripening and thickening of heavy cream. The cream we find in our markets is pasteurized without the natural bacteria and ferments added back to it, so *crème fraîche* is not a natural by-product. But the following recipe produces a *crème fraîche* that closely approximates the real thing. It should have the texture of whipped cream: smooth and thick but not too heavy. *Crème Fraîche* has a slightly tart, refreshing flavor and is excellent melted on cooked fish, or used instead of butter for broiling. Try it in sauces, or add fresh minced herbs, such as basil, dill, or tarragon, to *crème fraîche* for variety. Prepared *crème fraîche* and *crème fraîche* starter can also be purchased in specialty markets or the specialty food section of some grocery stores.

1 cup heavy cream
3 tablespoons buttermilk

In a clean glass jar with a tight-fitting lid, stir cream and buttermilk together.

Put in a warm place to ripen for 6 to 8 hours. Transfer to the refrigerator to chill and thicken. *Crème Fraîche* will keep up to 2 weeks in the refrigerator.

COCONUT CURRY SAUCE   Makes ¾ cup

Try this sauce with shrimp or scallops over rice.

1 tablespoon butter
1½ tablespoons curry powder
1 teaspoon minced fresh ginger
1 garlic clove, minced to a paste
¼ teaspoon ground cardamom
1 cup heavy cream
¼ cup coconut milk
1 tablespoon flaked coconut
6 fresh mint leaves, shredded
Salt and freshly ground pepper

Melt the butter in small saucepan and sauté the curry, ginger, garlic, and cardamom over low heat for 2 to 3 minutes. Set aside.

Meanwhile, cook the cream in a medium-sized saucepan over medium heat until it is reduced to ¾ cup. Stir in the coconut milk, flaked coconut, mint, and curry mixture. Simmer gently for about 5 minutes. Season to taste and serve.

CRAB SAUCE   Makes 1½ cup

This delicious shellfish sauce is excellent on angler, tilefish, sole, halibut, and lobster.

1½ cups heavy cream
2 tablespoons butter
½ teaspoon Dijon mustard
1 cup fresh lump crab meat
⅛ teaspoon cayenne
1 tablespoon minced fresh parsley
Salt and freshly ground white pepper to taste

In a small stainless steel saucepan, whisk the cream, butter, and mustard together. Simmer for 15 minutes, or until the cream is reduced and slightly thickened.

Stir in the crab meat, cayenne, and parsley. Heat through. Season with salt and pepper and serve.

MUSTARD SEED SAUCE   Makes ¾ cup

This tart sauce goes well with oily fish such as bluefish and mackerel, and is particularly good on broiled or grilled fish.

2 tablespoons prepared mustard with seeds
¾ cup heavy cream
1 tablespoon minced fresh parsley
1 heaping teaspoon minced fresh chives
Salt and freshly ground black pepper to taste

In a small stainless steel saucepan, combine the mustard and cream. Simmer for 5 minutes over low heat. Stir in the parsley and chives and season with salt and pepper. Serve immediately.

SORREL SAUCE   Makes ¾ cup

The tangy, lemony flavor of sorrel combines well with salmon, trout, shad, and swordfish.

1½ pounds fresh sorrel
2 tablespoons butter
½ cup heavy cream
1 teaspoon dry sherry
Salt and freshly ground black pepper to taste

Wash the sorrel in a sink filled with water and remove the stems. Pat the leaves dry and chop very coarsely.

Melt the butter in a stainless steel skillet. Sauté the sorrel leaves over low heat until wilted and falling apart. Add the cream and sherry and stir gently. Heat for 5 minutes but do not boil. Season with salt and pepper and serve immediately.

HORSERADISH CREAM SAUCE   Makes ¾ cup

A cold cream sauce, excellent for poached white fish or salmon.

½ cup heavy cream
1 heaping tablespoon prepared horseradish
1 teaspoon white wine vinegar
Pinch of ground nutmeg
Salt and freshly ground white pepper to taste

Whip the cream until it is slightly thick and smooth but not stiff. Blend in the horseradish, vinegar, and nutmeg, and season with salt and pepper.

PROVENÇALE SAUCE
Makes 2½ cups

An easy way to peel tomatoes is to drop them into simmering water for 5 seconds, then plunge them into cold water. The skins will slip right off.

2 tablespoons olive oil
2 garlic cloves, minced
1 large onion, chopped
¼ cup dry red wine
3 large ripe tomatoes, peeled, seeded, and chopped
1 fresh thyme, oregano, or marjoram sprig,
   or ½ teaspoon dried herb
Bay leaf
2 parsley sprigs, chopped
Salt and freshly ground pepper to taste

Heat the olive oil in a skillet and saute the garlic and onion until soft, about 7 minutes. Add the wine and reduce it slightly. Add the tomatoes, thyme, bay leaf, and parsley and cook over medium heat for about 10 minutes.

Remove the bay leaf, season to taste and serve.

BASQUE SAUCE
Makes a generous 2 cups

3 tablespoons olive oil
1 large red onion, chopped
2 garlic cloves, minced
2 anchovy fillets, chopped
¼ cup dry red wine
3 large ripe tomatoes, peeled, seeded, and chopped
8 large pitted black olives, chopped
1 fresh thyme sprig, or ½ teaspoon dried thyme
2 tablespoons chopped fresh parsley
Dash of cayenne (optional)
Salt and freshly ground pepper to taste

In a saucepan, heat the olive oil and sauté the onion and garlic in olive oil until soft, about 5 minutes. Add the anchovy fillets and saute 1 minute. Add the red wine, tomatoes, olives, thyme, parsley, and cayenne and simmer 10 minutes.

Remove the thyme sprig. Season with salt and pepper and serve.

SEAFOOD SAUCE
Makes 1 cup

This is our version of the familiar "cocktail sauce," famous as a dip for oysters, shrimp, and fried squid.

2 medium-sized ripe tomatoes, peeled, seeded,
   and chopped
2 tablespoons tomato paste
1 tablespoon red wine vinegar
2 tablespoons prepared horseradish
1 tablespoon minced celery
1 tablespoon minced onion
1 tablespoon olive oil
1 tablespoon capers, drained (optional)
3 tablespoons fresh lemon juice
1 small garlic clove, minced
1 teaspoon Worcestershire sauce
3 dashes Tabasco sauce, or to taste
Pinch of brown sugar
¼ teaspoon salt
⅛ teaspoon cayenne

Puree all the ingredients in a blender or food processor and chill.

FRESH TOMATO SAUCE WITH GREEN OLIVES
Makes 3 cups

Try this uncooked tomato sauce on hot or cold poached fish. It is also delicious with grilled fish.

5 large ripe tomatoes, peeled, seeded,
   and finely chopped
8 pitted green olives, sliced
½ cup virgin olive oil
Dash of red wine vinegar
1 green onion, finely chopped
2 garlic cloves, minced to a paste
8 large fresh basil leaves, shredded
2 tablespoons chopped fresh Italian parsley
Salt and freshly ground pepper

Combine all the ingredients in a glass bowl and blend well. Let the sauce stand 2 to 3 hours at room temperature before serving.

SEVICHE MARINADE

This marinade is for 1 pound of fish, which is enough for appetizers for four people. Use any firm white fish, or try scallops or shrimp. The hot chili pepper is optional, but to make it even hotter, leave in the seeds.

½ cup fresh lime juice
½ small red onion, chopped
1 fresh mild green chili such as Anaheim or *poblano*,
   sliced into rings
1 small hot chili such as *jalapeño* or *serrano*,
   seeded and sliced into rings
3 heaping tablespoons chopped fresh cilantro
1 small garlic clove, minced very fine
1 teaspoon olive oil
1 small tomato, seeded and chopped
Salt and freshly ground white pepper to taste

In a large glass or earthenware bowl, combine the fish with the lime juice, onion, chilies, 2 tablespoons of the chopped cilantro, garlic, and olive oil. Toss well. Cover the bowl with a clean cloth and put in a cool place to marinate for 2 to 3 hours. Toss occasionally. *Seviche* can also marinate covered in the refrigerator for 4 to 6 hours.

Just before serving add the tomato and the remaining 1 tablespoon of chopped cilantro, and season with salt and pepper. *Seviche* can be served with its marinade, or you can spoon it out with a slotted spoon. It will last 2 to 3 days covered in the refrigerator.

SPICY LIME/CILANTRO DIPPING SAUCE
Makes ½ cup

Excellent for fish dumplings or steamed whole fish.

Juice of 2 whole limes
2 teaspoons peanut oil
Dash of Asian sesame oil
Small pinch of sugar
1 tablespoon chopped fresh cilantro
½-inch piece of dried red pepper, sliced into rings

Mix all the ingredients together. Serve in individual bowls.

CHINESE DIPPING SAUCES

Use these flavorful sauces with steamed whole fish, fish dumplings, or plain poached fish. Serve them in individual bowls. Each recipe makes enough sauce for four people.

Cilantro-Orange

4 tablespoons rice vinegar or distilled white vinegar
1 tablespoon peanut oil
Dash of Asian sesame oil
1 tablespoon chopped fresh ginger
1 tablespoon chopped fresh cilantro
½ small orange, sliced
Black pepper

In a stainless steel or glass bowl, combine the vinegar, oils, ginger, and cilantro. Toss in the orange slices and add several grindings of black pepper. Allow to stand at room temperature for 15 minutes before serving.

Sweet and Sour Sauce

1 tablespoon rice vinegar or distilled white vinegar
2 tablespoons orange marmalade
1 teaspoon soy sauce
½ teaspoon peanut oil
1 teaspoon chopped fresh ginger

In a stainless steel or glass bowl, combine all the ingredients and blend well.

Hoisin Sauce

Hoisin sauce is a sweet and slightly spicy sauce made from soybeans, available in Chinese markets or the specialty section of some grocery stores.

3 tablespoons *hoisin* sauce
1 teaspoon rice wine vinegar or distilled white vinegar
Dash of Asian sesame oil

In a stainless steel or glass bowl, combine all the ingredients and blend well.

Green Onion, Ginger, and Garlic Sauce

1 tablespoon chopped green onion
1 teaspoon chopped fresh ginger
1 teaspoon chopped garlic
2 tablespoons soy sauce
2 tablespoons peanut oil
Pinch of brown sugar

In a stainless steel or glass bowl, combine all the ingredients and blend well.

Vinegar-Soy Sauce

Chili oil is regular oil (usually peanut) that has been infused with the flavor of a hot red chili. It is available in Chinese markets or in the specialty section of some grocery stores.

3 tablespoons cider vinegar
2 teaspoons soy sauce
Dash of chili oil or cayenne (optional)
1 tablespoon chopped green onion
Pinch of white pepper

In a stainless steel or glass bowl, combine all the ingredients and blend well.

SASHIMI DIPPING SAUCE   Makes 1 cup

Mirin is sweetened rice wine found in Japanese markets or the specialty section of some grocery stores. *Wasabi* is a very hot horseradish that comes in dried form in small tins.

1 tablespoon powdered *wasabi*
¼ cup soy sauce
1 tablespoon *mirin*

Blend 1 tablespoon of powdered *wasabi* with water, adding only a drop at a time, until it forms a paste.

Combine the soy sauce and the *mirin* and *wasabi* to taste.

WHITE PEPPERCORN VINAIGRETTE   Makes 1 cup

This vinaigrette is delicious spooned, peppercorns and all, over hot salmon, trout, or shad (or any white-fleshed fish). It is also great with cold poached fish. Crush whole white peppercorns with the back of a wooden spoon or in a mortar and pestle. Try adding tarragon or summer savory instead of chives.

1 tablespoon white peppercorns, barely crushed
1½ tablespoons white wine vinegar
¾ cup virgin olive oil
½ teaspoon Dijon mustard
⅛ teaspoon sugar
1 teaspoon minced fresh chives
Salt to taste

Combine the peppercorns and white wine vinegar in a medium-sized bowl. Set aside to marinate for 2 to 3 hours. Whisk the oil, mustard, sugar, and chives into the peppercorns until emulsified. Season with salt.

PINE NUT AND SWEET PEPPER RELISH   Makes 1 cup

This flavorful relish goes well with grilled fish, or with fish cooked *en papillote*.

1 yellow bell pepper
1 red bell pepper
⅓ cup pine nuts
1 tablespoon olive oil
1 teaspoon red wine vinegar
3 tablespoons minced onion
1 garlic clove, minced to a paste
1 teaspoon brown sugar
Large pinch of ground nutmeg
Pinch of salt
Several grindings fresh white pepper

To roast the peppers: Char the skins over a gas burner, on a grill, or under a broiler. The skin should be quite black all over. Place the peppers in a paper bag for 15 minutes to steam and cool. Stem and seed the peppers. Scrape the charred skin away with the blunt side of a knife; do not rinse. Chop the peppers and set aside.

Toast the pine nuts in a single layer on a baking pan in a preheated 375° oven for 5 to 7 minutes, or until light brown. Remove and cool. Coarsely chop two-thirds of the pine nuts and leave the other third whole.

Combine all the ingredients in a stainless steel or glass bowl. Blend well. Let stand 2 hours before using.

This relish will keep in a sealed jar for 1 week in the refrigerator.

SALSA

Makes 1½ cups

Salsa is great with grilled fish. For a spicy salsa, use *jalapeño* or *serrano* chilies, and to make it even spicier, leave in the seeds. For a milder salsa use a mild green chili such as Anaheim, *ancho, pasilla,* or Fresno. When handling any chilies, remember to wash your hands thoroughly after touching them, and avoid touching your eyes. Even the oil from mild chilies can irritate your eyes. Salsa will keep for up to 10 days in a sealed jar in the refrigerator.

> **2 large or 4 small ripe tomatoes, finely chopped**
> **1 small red onion, minced**
> **2 garlic cloves, minced**
> **Juice of 1 whole lime**
> **1 fresh mild green chili, minced, or ½ fresh hot green or red chili, seeded and minced**
> **8 fresh cilantro sprigs, chopped**
> **Pinch of sugar**
> **Salt and freshly ground black pepper to taste**

In a stainless steel or glass bowl, combine all the ingredients and blend well. Let the salsa stand 1 hour at room temperature.

SALSA VERDE

Makes 2 cups

Salsa verde is great with enchiladas, or over grilled fish or shellfish. When handling chilies, make certain not to touch your eyes or face, and wash your hands thoroughly afterwards. Add an extra half or whole hot chili to make the salsa very hot.

> **8 *tomatillos***
> **2 fresh mild green chilies such as Anaheim, *ancho,* or *poblano***
> **1 fresh small hot chili such as *serrano* or *jalapeño***
> **2 tablespoons oil**
> **2 garlic cloves, minced**
> **½ onion, chopped**
> **½ cup water**
> **2 teaspoons brown sugar**
> **¼ teaspoon salt**
> **10 fresh cilantro sprigs, chopped**

Pull the papery husks and the stems off the *tomatillos.* Wash them and pat dry. Slice each one in half. Slice the stems off the chilies, slice in half lengthwise and seed them. Brown the skins of the *tomatillos* and the chilies under the broiler for about 10 minutes. Finely chop the browned *tomatillos* and chilies.

Heat the oil in a large skillet. Sauté the garlic and onion for 3 minutes. Add the chopped *tomatillos,* chilies, water, brown sugar, and salt and cook over low heat for 15 minutes, stirring occasionally.

Remove the salsa from the heat, stir in the cilantro, and cool.

CAJUN SPICE MIX

Makes ¼ cup

Blend this dry spice mix into stews, or combine it with softened or melted butter for sautéing, grilling, or broiling.

> **1 tablespoon fennel seed**
> **1 tablespoon dried thyme**
> **1 tablespoon dried sage**
> **2 teaspoons paprika**
> **2 teaspoons onion powder**
> **1 teaspoon cayenne**
> **½ teaspoon garlic powder**
> **½ teaspoon cumin**
> **1 teaspoon freshly ground black pepper**

Grind or mince the fennel, thyme, and sage together until they become a powder. Combine with the other ingredients. Store in an airtight container.

Salade Niçoise

WHAT TO DO WITH COLD COOKED FISH

Salads and Spreads

We're all familiar with the ubiquitous tuna salad. More flavorful and fresher-tasting salads can be made with the fresh fish you cooked the night before, and fresh cooked tuna made into salad redefines the old standby.

Lean white-fleshed fish, whether poached, baked, grilled, broiled, or steamed, makes an excellent salad or spread. If first prepared with a sauce or relish, try making that an ingredient of the cold salad or spread and blend it right in.

When making salads, break the fish into large flakes, checking carefully for bones. Moisten it with a little mayonnaise, mustard, a dash of lemon juice, and season it with salt and pepper, and you have the basis for a salad. Add to this base salad different flavors, textures, and colors, such as minced onion, celery, mushrooms, or carrot. Curry and raisins, or grapes, chopped apple, and chopped walnuts added to cooked fish make two delightful summer salads that can be served in avocado halves. For a heartier fish salad, try adding cooked diced potato and onion. Spice the salad with a dab of horseradish and black pepper, and serve it with lots of toasted French bread. Broiled or grilled fresh tuna makes a fantastic *Salade Niçoise,* with steamed green beans, cooked new potatoes, tomatoes, olives, hard-cooked egg, lettuce, and anchovy, with a garlicky vinaigrette.

Leftover cooked shrimp, lobster, crab, or squid make great salads, prepared either with a mayonnaise dressing or with a vinaigrette. Leftover cooked clams or mussels can be marinated in oil, vinegar, mustard, salt, pepper, and herbs for a light snack with French bread.

Spreads are easily made by breaking the fish into flakes, removing all bones, and mincing it very fine. The minced fish can then be blended with mayonnaise or cream, seasonings, and anything from minced pimiento, caviar, or pickle to roasted nuts or chopped capers for a wonderful spread for crackers, black bread, and *baguette* slices.

CHAPTER 5

*Catch
of the
Day*

PAN-FRIED TROUT WITH SAGE

Baked Yams • Steamed Fresh Peas • Popovers
Dry White Wine

Serves 4

Trout has long been a favorite of sportfishermen, who seek them in lakes, rivers, and rushing mountain streams. Fishermen claim that the harder the living conditions for the trout, the better tasting it is, which in theory makes the highest mountain brook trout the most flavorful. The cultivated rainbow shown here is quite tasty in its own right, however, and is much more readily available.

Pan-fried Trout with Sage

Trout remains more moist and flavorful if you leave the bones in while cooking. When cooked properly, the bones will be very easy to remove as you eat the trout. When you have finished the top fillet, carefully lift out the entire bone structure, starting with the tail and loosening the bones as you go. It should come off virtually in one piece.

4 tablespoons Sage Butter, page 61
4 pan-dressed 8- or 9-inch trout
4 fresh sage sprigs
1 lemon, thinly sliced
¼ cup flour
Salt and freshly ground black pepper
2 tablespoons olive oil
4 tablespoons butter

Prepare the sage butter and store in the refrigerator until ready to use.

In the cavity of the trout, arrange sage sprigs and lemon slices. Dust each fish very lightly with flour and season lightly with salt and pepper. In a large heavy skillet, heat half the olive oil and half the butter over medium heat. Cook 2 trout for 3 to 5 minutes per side (depending on the size), or until the skin is browned and the flesh is opaque and flaking. Shake the pan gently as the fish is cooking to prevent it from sticking. Keep these trout warm while you cook the other 2 (or use 2 skillets), adding more oil and butter as needed.

Slice a tablespoon of sage butter onto each hot fish and serve.

Baked Yams

2 yams
3 tablespoons olive oil
Salt and freshly ground black pepper
1 teaspoon chopped fresh rosemary,
or ½ teaspoon dried rosemary

Preheat the oven to 375°.

Scrub (but do not peel) and thinly slice the yams. Rub the slices lightly with olive oil. Arrange in overlapping rows in an oiled casserole. Season with salt and pepper and sprinkle chopped rosemary on top.

Bake the yams in the preheated oven for 1 hour, or until they are quite tender when poked with a skewer.

Steamed Fresh Peas

The deliciously sweet flavor of fresh peas with butter and salt and pepper is enhanced by the simplicity of this dish. We like peas lightly cooked so they are still crunchy.

2 pounds fresh peas
1½ tablespoons butter
Salt and freshly ground white pepper

Shell the peas and rinse in cold water. Steam 2½ minutes. Toss with the butter and season to taste with salt and pepper.

Popovers

Makes 8 to 10

Preheat the oven *and* the pan for 10 to 15 minutes for the best results. Popover pans of heavy-gauge metal are preferred, and the ones with deep cups make tall, puffy popovers.

4½ tablespoons butter
3 eggs
1½ cups milk
¾ teaspoon salt
1½ cups unbleached all-purpose flour

Preheat the oven and popover pan to 450°.

In a small pan, melt 3 tablespoons of the butter and set aside. In a blender or food processor, blend the eggs. Add the milk, salt, and butter, blending between each addition.

With the blender or processor running, add the flour in ¼-cup portions. Blend until smooth.

Remove the hot pan from the oven. Drop a bit of the remaining 1½ tablespoons of butter into each cup. Pour batter into the hot buttered cups to fill each three-fourths full.

Bake popovers 15 to 20 minutes in the preheated oven, or until puffy and starting to brown. Reduce the heat to 400° and cook another 15 minutes.

Serve immediately with lots of butter and honey.

New England Steamed Clams

Fish Chowder • Green Bean Salad with Red Onions
Irish Soda Bread • Beer

Serves 6

Small soft-shell clams have been served so exclusively in their steamed form that they have earned the name "steamers," and in New England they are a classic shellfish meal. They are traditionally served along with their steaming broth and melted butter—the broth to douse the steamed clam meat in to rid it of any residual sand, and the warm butter for dipping. Eating steamers is wonderfully messy, so have lots of bread for soaking up butter and broth, and paper napkins for your fingers.

New England Steamed Clams

The best clams for steaming are, of course, steamers, but littleneck clams, as pictured here, or cherrystones can be substituted with excellent results. See page 16 for additional information about clams.

> **6 dozen clams**
> **Parsley Butter, page 61, melted**
> **½ cup dry white wine**
> **½ cup water**
> **4 garlic cloves, chopped**
> **2 shallots, chopped**
> **Bay leaf**
> **1 fresh thyme sprig, or a pinch of dried thyme**
> **6 peppercorns**

Scrub the clams under running water and soak in salted water for 1 hour.

Prepare the melted parsley butter and set aside in a warm place.

Place the clams in a deep kettle with the wine, water, garlic, shallots, bay leaf, thyme, and peppercorns. Steam over high heat, tightly covered, until all the clams are just open, anywhere from 3 to 10 minutes depending on the size and type of clam. Shake the pan from time to time to redistribute the clams. Do not overcook. Discard any that do not open. With a slotted spoon, remove the clams to large soup bowls or deep plates, reserving the cooking broth. Strain the broth through cheesecloth and pour it into small glasses, one for each serving. Pour the melted parsley butter into small dishes for each serving. To eat, lift each clam out of its shell by its black neck with a fork or your fingers. Dip it first in the broth, then in butter. It's messy, but it's worth it, and you can drink the clam juice after all the clams are gone.

Fish Chowder

Almost any white-fleshed fish can be used in this chowder. Try combining several types for a variety of flavors, such as haddock, cod, pollock, angler, plaice, or halibut. Buy whole fish and cut it up at home for this recipe is desired. Cooked and chopped shellfish can also be thrown into the pot.

> **1 pound fish bones and heads**
> **2 pounds white fish fillets, cut into bite-sized chunks**
> **5 cups water**
> **2 tablespoons diced salt pork or bacon**
> **4 tablespoons butter**
> **1 large onion, diced**
> **½ green bell pepper, seeded and finely chopped**
> **2 large potatoes, diced**
> **2 celery stalks, finely chopped**
> **2 garlic cloves, minced to a paste**
> **1 tablespoon fennel seeds**
> **Bay leaf**
> **1½ cups heavy cream**
> **Salt and freshly ground pepper**
> **Fresh dill sprigs**

In a large stockpot, gently boil the fish bones and heads in 5 cups of water, uncovered, for 30 minutes. Skim off the foam occasionally. Strain the stock through several layers of cheesecloth, discard the bones, and reserve the stock (you should have about 4 cups). Check the fish chunks carefully for bones and remove any with tweezers.

In a large pot, sauté the salt pork over low heat until golden. Remove the pieces of pork with a slotted spoon and reserve. Add 2 tablespoons of the butter to the pot. Increase the heat to medium-high and sauté the onion, green pepper, potatoes, celery, garlic, and fennel seeds until the onions are just golden, approximately 10 minutes.

Add the reserved stock and the bay leaf and bring to a boil. Reduce the heat, cover, and simmer for 10 minutes. Add the fish chunks and cook gently until white and flaky, approximately 3 more minutes. Stir in the cream, remaining butter, and reserved salt pork cracklings and reheat, but do not boil.

Season to taste with salt and pepper. Garnish each serving with a dill sprig and serve.

Green Bean Salad with Red Onions

> **2 pounds green beans**
> **1 red onion, thinly sliced**
> **8 pitted black olives, sliced into rounds**
> **¼ cup olive oil**
> **1 tablespoon white wine vinegar**
> **1 heaping teaspoon Dijon mustard**
> **1 garlic clove, minced to a paste**
> **   with a pinch of salt**
> **Salt and freshly ground black pepper**
> **4 parsley sprigs, chopped**

Rinse the beans under cold water and trim the ends.

Steam the beans until tender but still crunchy, approximately 5 minutes. Run them immediately under cold water and drain well. Pat dry.

In a salad bowl, toss the beans with the sliced onion and olives. Whisk the olive oil, vinegar, mustard, and garlic together and pour over the beans. Toss well to combine. Season to taste with salt and pepper, and place in the refrigerator to marinate for half an hour. Toss with the chopped parsley and serve.

BROILED BUTTERFLIED LOBSTER WITH MELTED BUTTERS

Warm Spinach Salad • Sliced Tomatoes • Italian Loaf
White Wine

Serves 2

It is hard to believe that lobster was once so abundant that the extras were used as bait for catching haddock and cod. But this creature has since been so zealously fished for its uniquely delicious sweet meat, that the price has soared as the population decreases. We serve our lobster dinner for two, to bring it into the realm of the possible. Lobster is also delicious boiled, steamed, or grilled in this recipe. We like our tomatoes drizzled with olive oil and sprinkled with a little cracked black pepper.

Broiled Butterflied Lobster with Melted Butters

Select the most active lobsters in the tank, and if possible, females (they contain not only the tomalley, but the flavorful coral as well, and are generally meatier). Lobster, after it has been killed, begins to deteriorate very quickly, so kill them just before cooking. See page 23 for information on handling live lobsters.

> **2 whole live lobsters, 1 to 1½ pounds each, cleaned**
> **and claws cracked**
> **Garlic Butter, page 61, melted**
> **Any or all of the following:**
> **Coral Butter (if the lobsters are female),**
> **page 61, melted**
> **Tomalley Butter, page 61, melted**
> **Chive Butter, page 61, melted**
> **Dill and Lemon Butter, page 61, melted**

To butterfly cleaned lobsters: Cut all the way through the hard shell of the tail up to the carapace (body), and curl each half up toward the claws. This exposes more of the tail meat for broiling.

Prepare the butters and keep in a warm place.

Preheat the broiler. Place the butterflied lobsters on a large baking sheet, brush with melted garlic butter, and broil flesh side up about 2 inches below the heating element. When the flesh is browning on top, the shell is bright red, and the meat is tender, the lobster is done. This takes approximately 12 to 15 minutes. You can also detach the carapace and claws from the tail for serving and present it right side up. Serve with the melted butters for dipping.

Warm Spinach Salad

> **1 pound fresh spinach**
> **3 bacon strips**
> **¼ red onion, thinly sliced**
> **6 mushrooms, thinly sliced**
> **1 garlic clove, peeled and slightly crushed**
> **2 tablespoons sherry vinegar**
> **3 tablespoon olive oil**
> **½ teaspoon Dijon mustard**
> **½ teaspoon sugar**
> **Freshly ground black pepper to taste**

Wash the spinach in a sink filled with water, changing the water several times. Stem the leaves by pulling the stem up the back of each leaf, from the base of the leaf to the tip. Dry the leaves thoroughly, tear in pieces, and place in a salad bowl.

Trim some of the fat off the bacon and dice it. In a skillet over medium heat, cook the bacon until crisp. Pour off half the fat, add the onion, mushrooms, and garlic and sauté briefly, until the mushrooms have just wilted. Discard the garlic. Remove the mushrooms, onions, and bacon bits and set aside.

Add the vinegar to the pan to deglaze it, scraping up the bits on the bottom with a wire whisk. Allow the vinegar to cook down for a few seconds, then add the oil, mustard, sugar, and pepper and whisk until emulsified.

Add the mushrooms, onions, and bacon to the spinach, and pour the hot dressing over them. Toss well and serve.

KEDGEREE

Homemade Sausage Patties • Orange Scones with Cream and Marmalade
Fresh Fruit • Hot Teas

Serves 6

Kedgeree is a British breakfast dish that has its origins in an Indian dish called *khichri,* a dish of rice with onion, egg, and butter. The British colonials added smoked fish, and made it their own *kedgeree.* It is tasty and filling, perfect for a cold winter morning. Try serving it with a sweet mango chutney on the side.

Kedgeree

This dish is traditionally made with smoked cod or haddock, but it can be made with other smoked fish as well, such as whitefish, salmon, tuna, or trout.

1 pound smoked cod or haddock
Milk Court Bouillon, page 59
6 tablespoons butter
1 small onion, thinly sliced
1½ cups unconverted long-grain rice
3 tablespoons curry powder
Seeds from 8 cardamom pods
⅛ teaspoon cayenne
Pinch of ground nutmeg
Bay leaf
½ pint heavy cream
4 hard-cooked eggs, chopped
½ cup raisins
6 green onions, minced, white part and
**   half the green**
⅓ cup coarsely chopped parsley
Salt and freshly ground black pepper

Poach the smoked fish in the milk court bouillon until it just begins to flake. Remove the fish with a slotted spoon and drain it on paper towels. Reserve the poaching liquid. Remove the skin, break the fish up into large flakes, check for bones, and set aside.

In a large pot, melt 4 tablespoons butter and sauté the onion for 5 minutes. Add the rice, curry, cardamom seeds, cayenne, and nutmeg and sauté the rice until it turns opaque, approximately 5 minutes.

Add the bay leaf, 1½ cups of the poaching liquid, and enough cold water to come up ½ inch above the surface of the rice. Bring the rice to a boil over high heat and continue to boil, uncovered, until the liquid is just below the surface of the rice, approximately 7 minutes. The surface should look pitted and bubbly. Cover with a tight-fitting lid and simmer 10 to 15 minutes more over *very* low heat. The rice should be quite dry and separated. Allow the rice to cool slightly with the lid off.

Remove the bay leaf from the rice. Over very low heat, mix the flaked fish, remaining 2 tablespoons butter, cream, three-fourths of the chopped hard-cooked eggs, raisins, green onion, and parsley into the rice. Heat gently, but do not cook. The kedgeree should be firm and moist. If too dry, add a little more cream or milk.

Season to taste with salt and pepper. Pile the kedgeree into a hot dish and sprinkle the remaining hard-cooked egg on top. Serve with chutney.

Homemade Sausage Patties

These sausages are easy because they don't need casings.

1 pound ground veal
½ pound ground pork
¼ pound fresh wild mushrooms (chanterelles,
**   morels, *cèpes,* or field mushrooms), minced**
1 egg, beaten
⅓ cup vermouth or dry white wine
1 tablespoon Dijon mustard
2 garlic cloves, minced to a paste
2 heaping teaspoons minced fresh sage,
**   or 1 teaspoon dried sage**
Pinch of ground cloves
Pinch of ground nutmeg
½ teaspoon of salt
½ teaspoon freshly ground black pepper
Butter for frying

Mix the veal and pork together in a bowl. Add all the remaining ingredients except the butter and mix well. Form the mixture into small patties and fry them in butter over medium-high heat for 7 to 10 minutes per side. Drain on paper towels and serve.

Orange Scones with Cream and Marmalade
Makes 12

2 cups unbleached all-purpose flour
3 teaspoons baking powder
1 tablespoon sugar
½ teaspoon salt
4 tablespoons butter
2 tablespoons fresh orange juice
Scant ½ cup milk or heavy cream
2 eggs
¼ cup currants
3 tablespoons grated orange zest
Sugar
Lime or orange marmalade
Sweetened whipped cream

Preheat the oven to 425°.

Combine the dry ingredients and sift them into a bowl. With a pastry cutter or two knives, cut in the butter until the mixture resembles coarse cornmeal.

Blend the orange juice, milk or cream, and 1 of the eggs together. Add slowly to the flour mixture, stirring gently until it forms a soft sticky dough that is not too wet. Mix in the currants and grated orange rind.

Turn the dough out onto a floured board, and with floured hands, knead it lightly until smooth, or no more than about 3 minutes. Divide the dough into 2 balls. Roll one out to a ¾-inch circle, and with a sharp floured knife, cut it like a pie into 6 wedges. Place the wedges on a greased cookie sheet, just touching each other. Repeat with the other ball of dough.

Lightly beat the second egg brush the tops of the scones with it. Sprinkle with sugar. Bake the scones in the preheated oven for 15 minutes, or until browned on top. Serve with lime or orange marmalade and whipped cream sweetened with powdered sugar.

MUSSELS MEDITERRANEAN

Hearty Green Salad • French Bread • Dry Red Wine

Serves 4

This classic dish is an easy and delicious Sunday night supper for four. Mussels are a relatively inexpensive shellfish, and are in season throughout most of the year except the summers on the West Coast (see "Red Tide," page 43). Beautiful green-lipped mussels from New Zealand are now available, as well as the small Atlantic blues and the large Pacific variety. Buy mussels from a reliable fishmonger.

Mussels Mediterranean

See page 24 for information on cleaning, soaking, and debearding mussels.

> **4 dozen mussels**
> **1 cup dry white wine**
> **4 garlic cloves, chopped**
> **Bay leaf**
> **4 shallots, chopped**
> **6 ripe Italian plum tomatoes,**
>   **pureed or finely chopped**
> **½ small dried red pepper (about a ½-inch piece),**
>   **seeded, or ⅛ teaspoon dried red pepper flakes**
> **8 fresh basil leaves, chopped,**
>   **or a large pinch of dried basil**
> **1 tablespoon olive oil**
> **Italian parsley, chopped**

Discard any mussels that are broken or do not close when the mussel inside is pricked. Scrub the shells and soak in salted water for 30 minutes. Pull off the long string that comes out of the shell (this is the beard).

Place the mussels in a large pot with the wine, garlic, bay leaf, and shallots. Bring the liquid to a boil over high heat and steam the mussels until they open, approximately 3 minutes. Shake the pot several times during steaming to allow some of the mussels on top to drop down to the bottom. With a slotted spoon, remove the mussels to a heated dish and cover to keep them warm. Discard any that do not open.

Add the tomatoes, red pepper, and basil to the stock. Bring the stock to a boil and reduce it for 2 minutes. Add the olive oil and blend.

Remove the top shell of each mussel and arrange the mussels in shallow soup bowls (or in one large serving dish). Add any mussel juice that accumulates back to the tomato sauce and heat. Pour some sauce over each serving and sprinkle chopped parsley on top.

Hearty Green Salad

> **¼ small head curly endive, or 8 leaves**
> **¼ head romaine**
> **¼ small head red leaf lettuce**
> **4 pitted black olives, sliced**
> **½ carrot, grated**
> **¼ cup crumbled feta cheese**
>
> *Vinaigrette:*
> **4½ tablespoons virgin olive oil**
> **1 tablespoon balsamic vinegar**
> **1 teaspoon Dijon mustard**
> **1 teaspoon minced green onion**
> **Small pinch of sugar**
> **Salt and freshly ground black pepper**

Wash and dry the endive, romaine, and red leaf lettuce. Tear the leaves into pieces and toss them in a salad bowl with the olives, carrot, and feta cheese.

Whisk the vinaigrette ingredients together and pour over the salad. Toss well and serve.

GRILLED THRESHER SHARK IN CORN HUSKS WITH TARRAGON BUTTER

Corn on the Cob • Grilled Carrots • Caesar Salad • Italian Red Wine

Serves 4

Thresher shark is a popular West Coast fish, while mako and blue sharks are common East Coast varieties. Shark is extremely low in fat, which is part of its popularity. It tends, however, to be a bit dry, and we find that cooking it inside corn husks holds in that essential moisture. The result is a succulent and delicately flavored piece of fish. Shark has an unusual metabolic system that causes it to have a slight ammonia odor when it is particularly fresh. The substance that causes the odor is absolutely harmless, but shark should be soaked in milk for an hour to neutralize it. We grill our carrots, rubbed with olive oil and lightly salted, until tender, about 20 minutes.

Grilled Thresher Shark in Corn Husks with Tarragon Butter

You can substitute tuna or swordfish in this recipe. Untrimmed corn yields the best husks since the long tops have not been lopped off. Use the slightly more tender inner corn husks for the wrappers.

4 shark steaks, ⅓ to ½ pound each
Milk
4 tablespoons Tarragon butter, page 61
24 to 30 fresh corn husks, about 8 inches long

Place the shark steaks in milk to cover to soak for 1 hour. Meanwhile, light the coals in a covered charcoal grill.

Prepare the tarragon butter and refrigerate until ready to use.

Soak the corn husks in water for 15 minutes.

Use 4 to 6 corn husks per piece of fish. Place 2 or 3 corn husks flat on a board in a cross shape. Put ½ tablespoon Tarragon Butter in the center of the cross, place one fish steak on top, and dot the top of the steak with another ½ tablespoon butter. Fold up the ends of the husk over the fish, place another 2 crossed husks on top and fold the ends under, forming a packet. Tear two ¼-inch strips from an inner corn husk and use it to tie the packet. Repeat these steps with the other 3 fish steaks.

Grill the packets over medium-hot coals, covered, 6 inches above the heat, for approximately 5 minutes per side. The husks will begin to char, which flavors the fish. To check doneness, peek inside one of the packets. With 2 forks, gently pry apart the flesh to see into the center of the fish steak. The fish should have just barely turned opaque through to the center, but should still be juicy and moist.

Corn on the Cob

Since the corn husks go around the fish, we put the corn on the grill, too. Pick out whole, untrimmed ears of corn with plump, even rows of pale yellow kernels.

4 corn cobs, untrimmed

Remove in whole pieces all but the last few pale green layers of corn husk. Without breaking them off, *gently* peel back the remaining husks of each ear to about 2 inches from the base. Pull off as much of the silk as possible. Rinse the corn and pull the husks back up over the ear.

Soak the ears in water for 15 minutes.

Shake off the excess water and grill the ears over medium-hot coals, 6 inches above the flame, turning several times, for 15 to 20 minutes. Serve with lots of butter and salt and pepper.

Caesar Salad

Croutons:
6 thick slices slightly stale French or Italian bread, cut into ½-inch cubes
3 tablespoons butter
3 tablespoons olive oil
1 garlic clove, slightly crushed
Small fresh rosemary sprig, or a pinch of dried rosemary

Dressing:
2 anchovy fillets
2 or 3 garlic cloves
¼ teaspoon salt
¼ cup olive oil
Juice of ½ lemon
1 teaspoon Dijon mustard
1 teaspoon Worcestershire sauce
1 egg yolk
5 tablespoons freshly grated Parmesan or Romano cheese
1 tablespoon capers, drained and crushed
2 small or 1 large head of romaine lettuce
Freshly ground pepper

To prepare the croutons, scatter the bread cubes on a baking sheet and crisp in a preheated 250° oven for 30 minutes. Heat the butter and olive oil in a skillet. Add the garlic clove and rosemary and sauté for 5 minutes over low heat. Remove the garlic. Increase the heat and sauté the bread cubes until brown and crisp. Drain on paper towels.

To prepare the dressing, mince the anchovies, garlic, and salt together on a cutting board until they form a paste. Place the paste in the bottom of a wooden salad bowl.

Add the olive oil, lemon juice, mustard, Worcestershire sauce, egg yolk, 3 tablespoons of the grated cheese, and capers. Whisk until well blended.

To prepare the greens, wash and thoroughly dry the leaves. Tear each leaf horizontally across the spine every 3 inches or so. Place the lettuce leaves in the wooden bowl containing the dressing and toss well.

Season generously with freshly ground black pepper, garnish with croutons, and sprinkle the remaining grated cheese on top.

CLAM AND MUSSEL PASTA

*Calamari Salad • Bruschetta • Romaine and Radicchio Salad
with Toasted Pine Nuts • Dry White Wine*

Serves 4

Seafood has a long tradition in Italian cuisine. Italy has many miles of coastline, and even inland cities are not very far from the coasts that abound with all different types of fish. Seafood is always prepared fairly simply in Italian cooking, so as not to disguise its freshness and flavor. This menu is inspired by the memory of several delicious meals in Positano, a small fishing village nestled into the steep shoreline of the Amalfi Coast.

Clam and Mussel Pasta

Select clams and mussels that are unbroken and tightly closed, or that close when pricked inside (see pages 17 and 24 for information on cleaning and soaking).

> **1 tablespoon salt**
> **1 pound dried spaghetti**
> **2 dozen littleneck clams, scrubbed and soaked**
> **2 dozen mussels, scrubbed, soaked, and debearded**
> **1 cup dry white wine**
> **⅔ cup virgin olive oil**
> **2 small garlic cloves, finely minced**
> **1 teaspoon dried red pepper flakes**
> **Fresh parsley, chopped**

Bring a large pot of water with 1 tablespoon of salt to a boil. Add the spaghetti and cook until firm but tender, approximately 7 minutes for dried pasta.

While the pasta is cooking, place the scrubbed and soaked clams and mussels in a large pot with the white wine. Steam them until they open, approximately 3 to 5 minutes. With a slotted spoon, remove those that open with to a bowl. Discard any that do not open. Shuck all but 6 clams and 6 mussels.

Put the oil, garlic, and red pepper flakes in a small saucepan and heat gently over low. Do not brown the garlic. Just before the pasta is done, remove the oil from the heat and add the shucked clam and mussel meats.

Drain the cooked pasta and toss with the hot oil and shucked clam and mussel meats. Arrange the remaining unshucked clams and mussels on top, sprinkle with parsley, and serve.

Calamari Salad

Take care not to overcook the squid or it will be tough. See page 31 for information on cleaning fresh squid.

> **1 pound squid, cleaned, bodies sliced into**
>   **½ inch rings, and tentacles reserved**
> **3 tablespoons virgin olive oil**
> **1 teaspoon red wine vinegar**
> **1 teaspoon fresh lemon juice**
> **1 ripe tomato, seeded and finely chopped**
> **6 parsley sprigs, chopped**
> **16 black olives (Greek or *niçoise*)**
> **1 green onion, sliced into rings**
>   **with half the green leaves**
> **Salt and freshly ground black pepper**

Bring a large pot of salted water to a boil. Drop the squid rings and tentacles into the boiling water and cook until the squid just loses its translucency, approximately 1½ minutes. Drain and run under cold water to cool. Pull off any remaining viscera attached to the rings (it will be a somewhat hard, jelled substance). Pat dry.

Blend the oil, vinegar, and lemon juice together in the bottom of a bowl. Add the tomato, parsley, olives, green onion, and squid and toss well. Season to taste with salt and pepper and marinate at room temperature for 1 hour (or 3 hours in the refrigerator) before serving.

Bruschetta

If you are grilling, try toasting the bread slices over the coals for a tasty grill-side snack. We've even indulged in this wonderful Italian garlic bread in front of the fire, toasting our bread on a grill held directly over the flames.

> **1 loaf Italian or French bread**
> **3 garlic cloves, peeled**
> **½ cup virgin olive oil**
> **Salt to taste**

Preheat the broiler.

With a serrated knife, slice the bread into ⅓-inch slices. Pour the olive oil into a shallow dish that is wider than the bread slices.

Toast both sides of the bread slices. When they are browned, remove and lightly rub one side of each slice with a raw peeled garlic clove. Quickly dip that side, face down, into the olive oil. Allow the slices to drain briefly on a plate, season with salt, and serve.

Romaine and Radicchio Salad with Toasted Pine Nuts

> **⅓ cup pine nuts**
> **1 small head romaine**
> **1 small head *radicchio***
> **6 to 8 large fresh basil leaves**
>
> *Dressing:*
> **4 tablespoons virgin olive oil**
> **1 tablespoon red wine vinegar**
> **Small pinch of sugar**
> **Salt and freshly ground white pepper to taste**

Toast the pine nuts in a single layer in a preheated 425° oven for 5 to 7 minutes. Remove and cool.

Wash and dry the romaine, *radicchio,* and basil leaves. Tear them into bite-sized pieces and set aside.

In the bottom of a salad bowl, whisk the oil, vinegar, sugar, and salt and pepper together. Place the romaine, *radicchio,* and basil leaves on top and toss just before serving. Sprinkle with the toasted pine nuts.

CAVIAR SMORGASBORD

Assorted Bread and Toast • *Seafood Tartlets* • *Mixed Nuts* • *Iced Vodka*

Serves 6

Caviar is a substance capable of turning the most staunchly practical into spendthrifts and epicureans, behavior undeniably justified by caviar's delicacy and flavor, its rarity, and its mystique. Our use of the word *smorgasbord* in this menu is a bit tongue-in-cheek because of the abundance it suggests, but it's a nice fantasy.

Caviar Smorgasbord

Our smorgasbord is a tasting of different caviars: pictured here are sevruga, beluga, and salmon and whitefish roe. The "true" caviars are made from the sturgeon, but we include caviar "substitutes" like the salmon and whitefish roes, which are excellent. Select your favorite or what falls into your budget and proceed. See page 15 for further information about caviar. Fresh caviar should be glistening and firm, with no dimples or a dry look. Good caviar demands to be eaten plain and simply — *without* lemon, chopped onion, chives, sour cream, or hard-cooked egg. Lesser-quality roes, however, such as lumpfish, can be improved with these toppings.

Serve caviar either in its original tin or in a small glass bowl nestled into cracked ice. Serve it with plain white bread trimmed, toasted, and sliced into triangles, or with dark brown bread, either toasted or plain. A small amount of cold *unsalted* butter may be spread on the toast or bread. The cold congealed butter keeps the caviar oil from saturating the bread or from draining off the caviar.

A pearl or bone knife or spoon is traditionally used to serve caviar, to prevent the caviar from taking on a metallic flavor. For the same reason, never serve caviar in a silver bowl. Serve caviar with ice-cold vodka or chilled champagne.

Seafood Tartlets

This recipe makes 6 to 8 individual tartlets or 1 large quiche.

Crust:
1½ cups unbleached all-purpose flour
½ cup (1 stick) cold unsalted butter, cut into ½-inch cubes
Pinch of salt
⅓ cup ice water

Filling:
8 medium-sized raw shrimp, shelled, deveined, and sliced in half
½ pound bay scallops, sliced in half
1 tablespoon dry white vermouth
3 tablespoons butter
3 shallots, minced
6 mushrooms, minced
3 eggs
1½ cups heavy cream
Pinch of ground nutmeg
4 large fresh basil leaves, cut into thin ribbons
1 tablespoon chopped fresh parsley
½ cup grated Gruyère cheese
¼ teaspoon salt
Freshly ground white pepper

To prepare the crust: Mound the flour on a large board or countertop. Make a well in the center and in it place the butter cubes and salt. With your fingertips, pinch the butter together with the flour and salt until the mixture resembles small corn flakes.

Sweep the mixture into a rectangle and make a trench down the middle. Add the ice water, 1 tablespoon at a time, tossing it with the flour after every addition. The dough should be moist but still very crumbly.

With the heel of your hand, press the dough, one section at a time, against the board to flatten it. When all the dough has been flattened once, fold it back together and flatten once more. Quickly shape the dough into a square and put it in the refrigerator, loosely covered, to rest for half an hour.

Divide the chilled dough in half, leaving the other half in the refrigerator. Roll out the dough on a floured board to a ⅛-inch thickness and cut it to the size of the tartlet pans. Press the dough into the pans and refrigerate until ready to use. Repeat with the other half of the dough. For 1 quiche pan, roll the dough out in one piece, press it into the pan, and refrigerate.

Just before preparing the filling, preheat the oven to 375° and prebake the pastry shells for 5 to 7 minutes, or until just barely beginning to brown. Allow the shells to cool before filling.

To prepare the filling: Preheat the oven to 375°. Toss the shrimp and scallops with the vermouth and set aside.

Melt the butter in a small skillet. Sauté the minced shallot and mushrooms over medium heat for 3 minutes, or until the mushrooms are wilted. Remove from heat and cool.

In a large bowl, beat the eggs and cream together. Add the mushrooms, nutmeg, basil, parsley, ¼ cup of the grated Gruyre, salt, and several grindings of pepper, and blend well. Separate the shrimp from the scallops and set aside. Add the scallops to the egg mixture and combine well. Pour some of the egg and scallop mixture into each pastry shell. Sprinkle the remaining ¼ cup of grated cheese over the tops and arrange two shrimp halves on the top of each tartlet.

Place the tartlets on a baking sheet and bake in the preheated oven for 20 to 25 minutes, or until the tops are puffed and brown and a knife inserted in the center comes out clean.

NEW-STYLE FISH AND CHIPS

Three-Color Slaw • Sweet and Sour Pickles • Lager

Serves 4

Fish and chips has long been a tradition in England, but not, as it may seem, since the dawn of time. The dish's origin was most probably coincidental with the invention of man-made, commercially used ice in the mid-1800s. With this ice, fresh fish could be transported from the coasts to the inland towns. Though the hot pie was then the quick hot meal of choice, fried fish quickly overtook it. Today fish and chips is still England's most ubiquitous fast food.

New-style Fish and Chips

Any firm white fish fillet can be used in this recipe. Select fillets that are small enough to turn easily with a slotted spatula. If necessary, cut larger fillets into smaller pieces. See page 51 for information on shallow- and deep-frying.

1¼ cups unbleached all-purpose flour
¼ teaspoon salt
1 egg, separated
½ cup beer
½ cup milk
Peanut or safflower oil for shallow- or deep-frying
2 pounds small cod or haddock fillets
Malt vinegar
Lemon wedges

Put 1 cup of the flour and the salt in a large bowl. Make a well in the center.

Beat the egg yolk with the beer and milk. Pour the liquid into the well in the flour and mix with a wire whisk. If more liquid is needed, add extra milk. Avoid overmixing the batter, but whisk until thick and smooth. The batter should be the consistency of heavy cream.

Beat the egg white until soft peaks form. Fold this gently into the batter, blending well.

Heat ¾ to 1 inch of oil over medium-high to high heat in a large, deep skillet, or use a deep-fryer or electric skillet heated to 375°. The oil is ready when a small cube of bread dropped into it crisps and browns within 1 minute.

Pat the fillets dry. Dust 1 fillet at a time with the remaining flour, and dip it into the batter, coating it evenly and well. Carefully lower 1 fillet at a time into oil, allowing the oil to reheat for a moment or two before adding another fillet. Fry 2 or 3 at a time (depending on the size of the fillets and your skillet—don't crowd the pan). Fry each on one side until it is *deep* golden brown, 4 to 5 minutes. Turn each fillet carefully, and avoid splashing hot oil or puncturing the batter casing. Fry on the other side until golden brown. Drain cooked fillets on paper towels, and place uncovered in a warm oven while you cook the rest. Serve with malt vinegar and lemon wedges.

Chips

These chips are, of course, otherwise known as French fries, but we bet you won't recognize the carrots! When you are making both fish and chips, we recommend you cook the chips first and keep them in a warm oven while you fry the fish in the same oil.

2 large potatoes, scrubbed
6 carrots, scrubbed and trimmed
Peanut or safflower oil for shallow- or deep-frying
Salt

Dry the potatoes and carrots well.

Slice the potatoes lengthwise into ⅜ by ⅜-inch slices, 3 inches long. Slice the carrots the same thickness and length. Heat ¾ to 1 inch of oil over medium-high to high heat in a large, deep skillet, or a deep-fryer or electric skillet heated to 375°. The oil is ready when a bread cube dropped into it crisps and browns within 1 minute.

Fry the potatoes and carrots in batches, and avoid crowding the pan. Move them around with a slotted spoon to keep them from sticking to each other. Cook both vegetables until the potatoes are golden brown, about 10 minutes. Remove them with the slotted spoon to paper towels to drain. Salt the chips to taste and place them in a warm oven while you fry the remaining chips.

Three-Color Slaw

½ cup Lemon-Dill Mayonnaise, page 59
½ small head green cabbage
¼ head red cabbage
½ head bok choy
½ red onion, thinly sliced into rings
Juice of ½ lemon
1 tablespoon sugar
½ teaspoon fennel seeds
Salt and freshly ground white pepper

Prepare the Lemon-Dill Mayonnaise and set aside.

Core the green and red cabbages. Slice them into very thin shreds. Rinse and pat dry the bok choy. Slice the leaves crosswise into thin shreds (the stems should be removed). In a large bowl, mix the cabbage, bok choy, and the onion together.

Blend the mayonnaise with the lemon juice, sugar, and fennel seeds. Pour just enough of this sauce over the shredded cabbages to coat evenly. Mix well (your hands are best for this).

Season to taste with plenty of salt and pepper and refrigerate for half an hour before serving.

SOLE MEUNIÈRE WITH CAPERS

Boiled New Potatoes with Parsley and Mustard • *Dilled Carrots*
Belgian Endive and Walnut Salad • *White Wine*

Serves 4

Delicately flavored sole is a fish that has been a favorite of Europeans, particularly the French, for centuries. According to the classic reference, *La Repertoire de la Cuisine,* there are over three hundred methods of preparing sole in classic French cuisine. *Meunière* means "miller's wife" in French, so-called because the soles are dredged in flour before sautéing. This dish is simple but classically elegant fare.

Sole Meunière with Capers

We vary our *sole meunière* a little by adding capers.

> ¼ cup unbleached all-purpose flour
> 4 sole fillets, ⅓ pound each
> Salt and freshly ground white pepper
> 6 tablespoons butter
> 1 tablespoon capers, drained
> Juice of 1 lemon
> Chopped fresh parsley

Put the flour on a plate. Sprinkle each sole fillet with salt and pepper and dredge lightly in the flour.

Heat 3 tablespoons of the butter over medium-high heat and sauté the fish until light golden brown on each side, approximately 2 to 3 minutes per side. Remove to a heated platter and keep warm in a very low oven.

Add the remaining 3 tablespoons of butter to the pan. Over medium heat allow the butter to foam and turn light brown. Whisk in the capers and lemon juice, and heat for 1 minute or so, until the foaming subsides. Pour over the fish, sprinkle with chopped parsley, and serve immediately.

Boiled New Potatoes with Parsley and Mustard

Try different flavored mustards with the potatoes, such as country-style, Dijon, or green peppercorn.

> 1½ pounds small new potatoes
> 2 tablespoons butter
> 1 heaping tablespoon prepared mustard
> 2 tablespoons chopped fresh parsley
> Salt and freshly ground pepper to taste

Wash the new potatoes but do not peel them. Slice each one in half.

Bring a large pot of water to a boil. Drop the potatoes into the boiling water and cook until tender when poked with a skewer, approximately 10 minutes.

Place the butter, mustard, and parsley in the bottom of a serving dish. When the potatoes are done, drain them and place them immediately in the serving dish. Toss them in the butter, mustard, and parsley, and season with salt and pepper.

Dilled Carrots

Pick out carrots that are fresh-looking and not cracked or wilted.

> 1¼ pounds baby carrots, or small carrots peeled,
>   sliced, and trimmed into 2-inch ovals
> 2 tablespoons butter
> 1 tablespoon heavy cream
> 1 teaspoon chopped fresh dill,
>   or ¼ teaspoon dried dill
> Salt and freshly ground white pepper

Trim and peel the carrots. Steam for 5 to 7 minutes, longer for larger carrots. The carrots should be crisp but tender when pierced with a skewer.

In a saucepan, melt the butter over medium heat. Add the carrots and sauté for 1 minute. Add the cream and dill and heat another 2 minutes.

Season to taste with salt and pepper and serve.

Belgian Endive and Walnut Salad

> ⅓ cup walnuts
> 1 head Belgian endive
> 4 tablespoons walnut oil
> 1 tablespoon champagne vinegar
> 1 heaping teaspoon orange marmalade
> 1 green onion, minced, white part only
> Salt and freshly ground white pepper

Toast the walnuts in a preheated 375° oven for 5 to 7 minutes, or until they are just beginning to darken slightly. Remove them and let cool.

Separate the leaves of the endive, rinse, and pat dry. Trim the blunt end.

In the bottom of a salad bowl, whisk together the walnut oil, vinegar, orange marmalade, and green onion and season to taste with salt and pepper. Place the endive leaves and walnuts on top and toss just before serving.

GRILLED STUFFED CALAMARI

*Skewered Root Vegetables • Spinach Fettuccine and Fresh Tomato Sauce with
Green Olives
Tender Greens Salad • White Wine*

Serves 4

Calamari, or squid, is an unusual shellfish in every way. Its peculiar shape lends itself to many different cooking methods, and its mild flavor can be combined with a variety of ingredients. Its long tubular body is perfectly suited to stuffing: it holds together while cooking and delicately flavors the stuffing. Squid also makes an interesting and different presentation.

Grilled Stuffed Calamari

Look for squid with bodies 4 to 5 inches long. If the squid has already been cleaned by the fishmonger and the tentacles have been discarded, buy a few extra squid to chop for the stuffing.

> 1 pound squid, cleaned (see page 31)
> Garlic Butter, page 61, melted
> 1 small eggplant
> Salt
> 3 tablespoons olive oil
> 2 garlic cloves, minced
> ¼ cup bread crumbs
> ¼ cup grated Parmesan cheese
> 1 egg, well beaten
> 1 tablespoon fresh chopped oregano, or 1 teaspoon
>   dried oregano
> Salt and freshly ground black pepper to taste

Wash the cleaned squid inside and out under cold running water, then pat dry. Put the tentacles and bodies in separate bowls and refrigerate both until ready to use.

Prepare the melted garlic butter and set aside in a warm place.

Slice the eggplant into ⅛-inch rounds and place them on a layer of paper towels. Salt the slices lightly and allow them to drain for 30 minutes.

While the eggplant is draining, light the coals in a charcoal grill.

Press the salted eggplant slices with paper towels to remove excess moisture. In a large skillet over medium heat, heat ½ tablespoon olive oil. Fry the eggplant slices in batches until well browned, adding a little oil when needed. Drain the slices on paper towels.

Finely chop the eggplant. Finely chop the reserved tentacles (or extra bodies). Combine the eggplant and chopped squid in a bowl with the garlic, bread crumbs, Parmesan cheese, egg, and oregano, and season with salt and pepper.

Stuff 1 tablespoon of stuffing into each squid shell. Do not overstuff since the squid shrinks during cooking and the stuffing expands. If the squid bodies are small, secure the opening with a toothpick. Brush the squid with melted garlic butter and grill over medium-hot coals, turning frequently, until they are browned and firm and the stuffing is cooked, approximately 10 to 12 minutes.

Skewered Root Vegetables

> 8 small French carrots
> 8 baby turnips, ends trimmed (or 2 small ones
>   quartered)
> 8 baby pattypan squash (or 4 small ones sliced in
>   half)
> 8 tiny onions, trimmed
> Olive oil
> Salt and freshly ground black pepper to taste

Soak 6 wood skewers in water for 15 minutes.

Wash the carrots, trim the green tops to 1½ inches, and pat dry.

Wash the turnips and squash, pat them dry, and peel the onions.

Rub the vegetables with olive oil and skewer them. Sprinkle them with salt and pepper and grill over medium-hot coals until tender when poked with a skewer, approximately 20 minutes.

Spinach Fettuccine and Fresh Tomato Sauce with Green Olives

The delicate flavor of this uncooked tomato sauce goes well with fresh spinach pasta cooked *al dente*.

> Fresh Tomato Sauce with Green Olives, page 65
> 1 tablespoon salt
> ¾ pound spinach *fettucine*, preferably fresh
> Grated Parmesan cheese

Prepare the Fresh Tomato Sauce and set it aside.

In a large pot, bring plenty of salted water to a boil. Immerse the pasta and cook it, stirring occasionally to separate the strands, for approximately 4 minutes for fresh pasta or 8 to 10 for dried. Drain it well, toss with Fresh Tomato Sauce, and serve with plenty of grated Parmesan cheese on the side.

Tender Greens Salad

> 1 small head limestone lettuce
> ½ head butter lettuce
> 8 fresh basil leaves
> 4 tablespoons virgin olive oil
> 1 tablespoon white wine vinegar
> Salt and freshly ground pepper

Gently rinse and dry the lettuce and basil leaves. Tear the lettuce leaves in half and toss them together with the basil leaves.

Combine the olive oil and vinegar in the bottom of a salad bowl. Season the mixture with salt and pepper. Put the salad greens on top and toss them just before serving.

PRAWNS WITH COCONUT CURRY SAUCE

Crab Dumplings • Steamed Basmati Rice • Snow Pea Salad
Beer

Serves 4

The flavors in this menu are an borrowed from modern Thai cuisine, which combines the unusual herbs and spices indigenous to Southeast Asia with the lightness and delicacy of European cooking. Though never colonized by any European nation, the kingdom of Siam was often visited by European travelers, and its cuisine was influenced by the neighboring Dutch- and French-settled countries.

Prawns with Coconut Curry Sauce

The terms "prawn" and "shrimp," though technically descriptive of different creatures, are used interchangeably. They are generally considered indications of size, hence jumbo shrimp are often called prawns.

> **12 to 16 raw fresh prawns (or medium to large shrimp), peeled and deveined (see page 29)**
> **Coconut Curry Sauce, page 63**
> **4 tablespoons butter**
> **1 green onion, white part only, chopped**
> **2 cilantro sprigs, chopped**

Rinse the prawns under cold water and pat dry.

Make the Coconut Curry Sauce and set it aside in a warm place.

In a large skillet over medium heat, melt the butter and sauté the green onion and prawns until the prawns are just pink and opaque, 3 to 5 minutes.

Turn the heat to low and add the sauce to the skillet with the prawns. Heat through.

Serve over rice and sprinkle chopped cilantro on top.

Crab Dumplings

Dumpling wrappers, often called *gyoza* or won ton skins, can be found in Asian specialty markets or in the refrigerated section of some grocery stores. They come round or square, in packets containing approximately 4 dozen individual wrappers that have been lightly floured so they won't stick together. Thai hot sauce, a red chili paste, is also available in specialty markets.

> **Spicy Lime-Cilantro Dipping Sauce, page 65**
> **¾ pound (2 cups) fresh lump crab meat**
> **1 green onion, white part and half the green leaves, minced**
> **1 garlic clove, minced to a paste**
> **1½ tablespoons chopped cilantro**
> **1 teaspoon soy sauce**
> **1 teaspoon Thai hot sauce (*nam prik*)**
> **½ teaspoon minced fresh ginger**
> **1 tablespoon sesame seeds**
> **1 egg, well beaten**
> **2 dashes of Asian sesame oil**
> **24 to 26 dumpling wrappers**

Prepare the dipping sauce and set it aside.

Combine the crab meat with the green onion, garlic, cilantro, soy, hot sauce, ginger, sesame seeds, egg, and sesame oil. Mix well.

Place one wrapper flat on a work surface. Dip your index finger in water and lightly moisten the edge of the wrapper all the way around. Place a dollop of stuffing in the center. Fold the wrapper over so the edges meet, and pinch the edges closed, making a few small tucks to seal them, or press with a fork.

Place the dumplings on a sheet of waxed paper until all are ready.

Bring a large pot of water to a boil. Drop the dumplings in one at a time. Gently agitate the water to prevent the dumplings from sticking to the pan or to each other.

Cook the dumplings until they float and are wrinkly, approximately 6 minutes. Remove them with a slotted spoon and strain.

Serve hot with Spicy Lime-Cilantro Dipping Sauce.

Steamed Basmati Rice

Basmati rice is an aromatic long-grain Indian rice found in Indian specialty markets.

> **2 cups Basmati rice**
> **Water**

Put the rice in a large pot. Wash and strain it in four changes of water, or until the water is clear. After pouring off the last rinsing water, put enough water in the pot to come up to a level ½ inch above the top of the rice.

Over high heat, bring the rice to a boil. Reduce the heat to medium-high and continue boiling, uncovered, until all the water on the surface is absorbed, approximately 7 minutes. The surface should be pitted and bubbly.

Cover the pot with a tight-fitting lid and reduce the heat to as low as possible. Simmer for another 10 to 15 minutes, or until the rice is dry and fluffy. Do not allow the rice to burn.

Snow Pea Salad

Look for bright green, tender, young snow peas—large, older ones are too fibrous.

> **½ pound snow peas**
> **2 tablespoons oil, preferably peanut or safflower**
> **1 teaspoon chunky peanut butter**
> **1 teaspoon rice vinegar or distilled white vinegar**
> **1 teaspoon light soy sauce**
> **1 green onion, white part only, minced**

Wash the snow peas and remove any strings. Steam the peas for 2 minutes, or until bright green but still crunchy. Run them immediately under cold water to cool. Pat dry. Combine the oil, peanut butter, rice vinegar, soy, and green onion. Whisk to emulsify. Arrange the snow peas on a platter and drizzle the dressing on top.

RED SNAPPER IN A CLAY BAKER
WITH BASQUE SAUCE

Spinach with Currants and Pine Nuts • Eggplant with Yogurt-Mint Dressing
Saltless Italian Bread • Dry Red Wine

Serves 4

Clay bakers are excellent for cooking fish. They are soaked in water before cooking, which creates steam inside the baker and holds in moisture. Thus the fish stays moist without cooking in liquid. The sauce also heats inside the baker, and its aroma and flavor permeate the fish as it cooks.

Red Snapper in a Clay Baker with Basque Sauce

Red snapper on the West Coast is more often rockfish posing as red snapper. Though not as delicately flavored as "true" red snapper, it can be substituted in this recipe. (Incidentally, red snapper flown in from the East Coast will be labeled "true red snapper.") Nearly any firm, lean white-fleshed fish will cook beautifully in a clay baker.

2 large red snapper fillets, approximately ¾ pound each
Basque Sauce, page 65

Preheat the oven to 450°.

Prepare the Basque Sauce and set it aside in a warm place. Place the clay baker in a sink of water to soak for 10 minutes.

Arrange the fillets in the clay baker, pouring the warm sauce between the layers and over the top.

Cook in the preheated oven for 20 minutes, or until the fish is flaking and has lost its translucency.

Spinach with Currants and Pine Nuts

2 pounds fresh spinach
6 bacon slices
2 tablespoons butter
1 garlic clove, slightly crushed
2 tablespoons pine nuts
2 heaping tablespoons currants
Salt and freshly ground black pepper to taste

Wash the spinach in several changes of cold water in a deep sink. Pull the stem up and off the back of each leaf by pulling up from the base to the tip of the leaf.

Without drying the leaves, place the spinach in a large pot. Cover and steam the spinach over high heat until the leaves are just wilted, approximately 2 minutes. Remove from the pan with a slotted spoon and place in a sieve. Press the excess moisture out with paper towels and chop coarsely.

In a skillet, sauté the bacon until crisp and discard (or reserve to crumble over the finished dish, if desired). Pour off all but 2 tablespoons of the fat and add the butter. Sauté the garlic, pine nuts, currants, and several grindings of pepper over medium heat until the pine nuts are just beginning to turn golden. Remove the garlic. Add the chopped spinach and stir until the spinach is heated through. Season with salt pepper and serve.

Eggplant with Yogurt-Mint Dressing

This dish can be prepared in advance since it is best served at room temperature.

1 large eggplant
Salt
Olive oil
Generous ½ cup plain yogurt
Juice of ¼ lemon
2 teaspoons virgin olive oil
½ teaspoon ground fenugreek
1 heaping tablespoon finely chopped fresh mint
½ teaspoon sugar
Freshly ground white pepper to taste
Fresh mint leaves for garnish

Slice the eggplant into ⅛-inch rounds. On several sheets of paper towels, arrange the eggplant slices in one layer. Lightly salt the slices, and repeat the layering until all the pieces are salted. Allow the eggplant to drain for half an hour. After the eggplant has drained, press the slices with clean paper towels to remove the excess moisture.

In a large skillet, heat just enough olive oil to barely cover the bottom. Over medium heat, brown the eggplant slices well on both sides. Work in batches, adding a little olive oil to the pan when needed.

Arrange the cooked eggplant on a platter and set it aside to cool.

Blend the yogurt, lemon juice, olive oil, fenugreek, mint, sugar, and pepper. Drizzle the dressing over the eggplant and arrange mint leaves on top.

SEAFOOD JAMBALAYA

Crispy Okra • Corn Bread Muffins • Chicory Salad with Toasted Pecans
Beer

Serves 6

The Acadians—as the early French settlers of Nova Scotia called themselves—lived a relatively quiet farming life in the New World until the British forced them out in the 1700s. Dispersed and homeless, these expatriate French were drawn to French-dominated Louisiana. Though Louisiana was at the time ruled by Spain, the Acadians, or "Cajuns," as the American Indians called them, stayed, and the mispronounced name stuck. Over the years their cuisine, based on French farm cooking but influenced by the Spanish and the American Indians in the region, developed into a delicious and eclectic blend of flavors and spices.

Seafood Jambalaya

"Jambalaya" is thought to be derived from a Spanish dish, but it is more likely that the word comes from the French word *jambon,* for ham, which is traditionally a component of the dish. The Spanish influence, however, is certainly in evidence.

4 teaspoons Cajun Spice Mix, page 68
8 live crayfish
6 thick bacon slices, diced
8 large raw shrimp, heads and shells intact
¼ pound bay scallops
1 pound white fish fillets, cut into bite-sized pieces
  and bones removed
Olive oil
1 large onion, coarsely chopped
1 green bell pepper, coarsely chopped
1 red bell pepper, coarsely chopped
3 garlic cloves, minced
2 cups unconverted long-grain white rice
4 medium tomatoes, chopped
4 cups White Wine Fish Stock, page 58
2 cups water
1 tablespoon brown sugar
¼ teaspoon cayenne
4 large crab claws, cooked and cracked
Salt and freshly ground pepper
3 green onions, chopped
8 parsley sprigs, chopped

Prepare the spice mix and set aside.

Bring a pot of water to a boil. Immerse the live crayfish in the boiling water and cook for 2 minutes. Remove and set aside to cool.

In a large stockpot, cook the bacon until crisp. Remove it to paper towels with a slotted spoon to drain and set aside.

Over medium-high heat, sauté the shrimp, scallops, and white fish one at a time in the bacon drippings, removing to paper towels to drain. Add a little olive oil if needed. The shrimp will cook in approximately 2 minutes (until opaque), the scallops in 1 to 1½ minutes (until firm), and the fish in 2 minutes (until firm).

When all the seafood is cooked, add the onion, peppers, and garlic to the bacon drippings and sauté over medium-high heat for 5 minutes. Add a little olive oil if needed. Add the rice and sauté until opaque.

Add the tomatoes, fish stock, water, Cajun spice mix, brown sugar, cayenne, and reserved bacon pieces. Simmer uncovered and undisturbed over low until the rice is nearly done and about ½ inch of liquid remains, approximately 20 minutes. Fold in all the seafood, including the crab claws, cover, and cook another 10 minutes.

Season to taste with salt and pepper. Pile into a large dish, sprinkle chopped green onions and parsley on top, and serve.

Crispy Okra

1 pound fresh okra, washed and trimmeed
½ cup milk
1 egg
1 cup breadcrumbs
4 tablespoons butter, melted
Salt and freshly ground white pepper to taste

Preheat oven to 475°.

Drop the okra into a pot of boiling water and blanch for 1 minute. Drain and pat dry.

Whisk the milk and egg together in a bowl. Place the breadcrumbs in another bowl. Dip the okra into the egg and then into the bread crumbs (try not to get the breadcrumbs soggy as you work by using only one hand for each bowl). Place the breaded okra on a baking sheet. Using a brush, lightly dab the okra with melted butter. Season with salt and pepper. Bake in the preheated oven until brown, about 10 minutes.

Corn Bread Muffins

Makes 12

This batter can also be used for one pan of corn bread. Increase the cooking time to 20 minutes, or until a skewer inserted into the center comes out clean.

1 cup yellow cornmeal
¾ cup unbleached all-purpose flour
⅓ cup dark brown sugar
2 teaspoons baking powder
1 teaspoon baking soda
¼ teaspoon salt
1 large egg
½ cup milk
¾ cup creamed corn
1 tablespoon butter, melted

Preheat the oven to 425°. Generously grease a 12-cup muffin tin.

In a large bowl, combine the cornmeal, flour, brown sugar, baking powder, baking soda, and salt.

In another bowl, beat the egg together with the milk, creamed corn, and melted butter. Stir this into the cornmeal mixture until well blended.

Spoon the mixture into muffin cups to three-fourths full. Bake at in the preheated oven for 15 minutes, or until the tops are browned and a skewer inserted in the center of a muffin comes out clean.

POACHED ANGLER WITH CRAB SAUCE

Leek and Potato Pancakes • Pineapple, Avocado, and Papaya Salad • Dry White Wine

Serves 4

Angler, also known as monkfish, is a strange and fascinating fish. Its huge head and jaw form a large trap for delicious crustaceans such as crab, shrimp, and squid. The angler sports its own rod and reel: a long flexible spine that juts out from its top fin, at the end of which is a shiny translucent tip. The angler dangles this shiny bait in front of its gaping mouth. When a curious crustacean gets near it, the angler thrusts forward with its powerful tail and catches its prey. This shellfish diet makes the angler flavorful, and it is often compared with lobster in both texture and taste.

Poached Angler with Crab Sauce

Tilefish has a diet similar to the angler's, and is therefore similar in flavor.

Crab Sauce, page 63
1½ pounds angler or tilefish fillets
Milk Court Bouillon, page 59
2 parsley sprigs, chopped

Prepare the crab sauce and set aside in a warm place.

Place the angler fillets in a large pan on top of the stove. Pour the court bouillon over the fish and add enough water to just cover. Remove the fillets with a slotted spoon and bring the court bouillon to a boil. Reduce the heat to a very low simmer and lower the fillets back into the pan. Cover and poach until the fillets lose their translucency, approximately 7 minutes for a ¾-inch thickness.

Remove the fish to a platter with a slotted spatula and spoon the crab sauce over the fish. Sprinkle chopped parsley on top.

Leek and Potato Pancakes

Grated potato will darken very quickly, so plan on cooking these pancakes immediately after preparing the mixture. Whole peeled potatoes will keep in a bowl of cold water, but be sure to dry them well before grating.

2 medium-sized potatoes
2 leeks, white part only
2 tablespoons flour
1 egg, separated
¼ cup heavy cream
1 heaping teaspoon minced fresh rosemary, or ½ teaspoon dried rosemary
1 tablespoon chopped fresh parsley
Salt and freshly ground pepper to taste
3 tablespoons butter
3 tablespoons oil

Peel the potato and grate it with a medium grater. Spread the potato on a layer of paper towels, then place paper towels on top and press to remove excess moisture.

Grate the leeks. Put the drained potatoes and leeks together in a bowl and toss with the flour.

Whisk the egg yolk, cream, rosemary, and parsley together.

Pour over the leeks and potatoes and mix well. Sprinkle with salt and pepper.

Whip the egg whites until soft peaks form and gently fold them into the potato and leek mixture.

In a large skillet, heat 1 tablespoon butter and 1 tablespoon oil over medium-high heat. Drop a large dollop of pancake mixture (about 3 tablespoons) into the pan and flatten. Repeat until the pan is full. Fry on each side until crisp and brown, approximately 5 minutes per side. Repeat with the remaining mixture, adding more oil and butter to the pan as needed.

Drain the pancakes on paper towels in a warm oven until all have been cooked.

Pineapple, Avocado, and Papaya Salad

½ fresh pineapple
1 avocado
1 papaya
½ lemon
Salt and freshly ground black pepper to taste

Peel and slice the pineapple into half rounds. Reserve the top.

Peel, seed, and slice the avocado into sections.

Peel, seed, and slice the papaya into sections.

Arrange the fruit and pineapple top on a platter and squeeze lemon juice over the avocado and papaya. Sprinkle salt and pepper on the avocado and papaya.

HALIBUT BAKED IN PARCHMENT WITH PINE NUT AND SWEET PEPPER RELISH

Baked Fennel and Turnips with Cream • Orange Salad on Watercress
French Bread • Dry White Wine

Serves 4

Baking in a parchment packet, known as *en papillote* in French cuisine, is an excellent way to cook fish. The parchment, when properly sealed, puffs up in the hot oven. The fish cooks in its own juices inside this "steaming chamber" and remains very moist and succulent. The slightly sweet relish in our recipe lightly flavors the fish and is hot and aromatic when guests break open their own packets.

Halibut Baked in Parchment with Pine Nut and Sweet Pepper Relish

Any firm white-fleshed fish, such as black sea bass, red snapper, Chilean sea bass, flounder, grouper, or tilefish may be substituted for the halibut in this recipe. Use one fillet per serving if small fillets are unavailable, or cut the larger ones in half.

Pine Nut and Sweet Pepper Relish, page 66
Butter
Salt and freshly ground white pepper
**8 small halibut fillets, approximately ⅓ pound
      per serving, boned**
White wine

Prepare the relish a few hours in advance and set aside. Preheat the oven to 375° (this step is important, as steaming should begin the moment the packets are placed in the oven). Fold a piece of parchment in half lengthwise and cut out half of a heart with the center at the fold. Open the paper (you should now have a whole heart) and butter one half. Lightly salt and pepper that same half and place 1 fillet on it. Spread 1 tablespoon of the relish over the fillet and place another fillet on top. Dot the top fillet with butter, spread another 1 tablespoon of relish on top, and sprinkle a teaspoon or so of white wine over it. Season lightly with salt and pepper.

Fold the other half of the paper over so the edges meet. Starting at the top center of the heart, fold the edges together in small overlapping folds, working your way down to the bottom point. Fold the bottom under twice so that no moisture will leak out. It is important for the packets to be well sealed. Repeat these steps with the other 3 packets. Place the packets on a baking sheet and bake in the preheated oven for 10 to 12 minutes. Remove the packets from the oven. Cut a small hole at the corner of each one and drain off the liquid without crushing or tearing the packets.

Serve the packets immediately on large plates and let each diner open his or her own.

Baked Fennel and Turnips with Cream

The flavors of fennel and turnips mellow and mingle in this delicious, creamy dish.

**1 large fennel bulb, white part only
   (reserve some leaves for garnish)**
2 medium-sized turnips
1 tablespoon butter
¾ cup heavy cream
1 teaspoon Dijon mustard
1 tablespoon chopped fresh chervil or parsley
Pinch of ground nutmeg
Salt and freshly ground white pepper

Preheat the oven to 375° and butter a shallow baking dish.

Wash and trim the fennel and turnips, and peel the turnips. Slice the turnips into ⅛-inch-thick rounds. Slice the fennel vertically into ⅛-inch-thick slices. Alternating fennel and turnip slices, arrange them in overlapping rows in the buttered dish. Dot with butter.

Whisk the cream, mustard, chervil, and nutmeg together and pour over the fennel and turnips. Sprinkle with salt and pepper.

Cover the dish with aluminum foil and bake in the preheated oven for 30 minutes. Remove the foil and bake uncovered another 20 minutes, or until the turnips are tender when poked with a skewer and the top is brown and bubbly. Sprinkle the reserved fennel leaves on top and serve.

Orange Salad on Watercress

This may be one of the most refreshing salads around.

1 garlic clove, slightly crushed
4 oranges (blood oranges if available)
1 green onion, including half the green leaves
16 black olives (Greek or *niçoise*)
1½ tablespoons virgin olive oil
Freshly ground black pepper to taste
1 bunch watercress
Salt to taste

Rub a salad bowl with the crushed garlic and set aside, leaving the garlic in the bowl.

Score the rind of the oranges 6 times from top to bottom (this makes them easier to peel). Pull off the scored skin, then trim off any thick white peel remaining. Do not pierce the oranges.

With a sharp knife, slice the oranges crosswise into ¼-inch-thick rounds. Cut each round in half and place in the salad bowl. Remove any seeds as you work.

Slice the green onion into thin rounds and sprinkle over the oranges along with the olives. Pour the oil over the oranges, sprinkle with plenty of freshly ground black pepper, and toss gently to mix.

Allow the salad to marinate for half an hour. Rinse the watercress and arrange it on a plate. Just before serving, remove the garlic clove, season the oranges with salt, and toss again gently. Arrange the salad on top of the watercress and serve.

POACHED SALMON WITH WHITE PEPPERCORN VINAIGRETTE

Herbed Rice with Mushrooms • Oven-roasted Summer Squashes
French Bread • White Wine

Serves 4

Many people consider salmon their favorite fish. It retains its beautiful pinkish-orange color when cooked, and has a delicate texture and exquisite flavor. Salmon was once an abundant fish in American waters, but unfortunately overfishing and pollution have drastically reduced its numbers. Regulations on fishing for salmon have become rather strict in an effort to build the population, but it will probably never reach the numbers it once did.

Poached Salmon with White Peppercorn Vinaigrette

This recipe comes from Midge May, a Los Angeles caterer who specializes in healthy gourmet meals.

White Peppercorn Vinaigrette, page 66
1 bunch watercress
4 salmon steaks
Court Bouillon, page 58

Prepare the White Peppercorn Vinaigrette and set it aside to marinate for 1 hour. Rinse and pat dry the watercress and set aside.

Preheat the oven to 450°. Place the salmon steaks in an ovenproof dish. Heat the court bouillon, pour it over the fish and add enough hot water to just cover. Cover the dish with aluminum foil and place in the preheated oven.

Poach the fish for approximately 10 minutes for 1-inch steaks, or until the fish flakes and is opaque in the center.

Arrange the watercress on a platter. With a slotted spatula, remove the fish to the platter. Spoon the vinaigrette over the hot fish and serve immediately.

Herbed Rice with Mushrooms

Use any fresh or dried wild mushroom, such as chanterelles, morels, *porcini*, or *cépes*, in this attractive and flavorful rice.

2 cups unconverted long-grain white rice
3 tablespoons butter
¼ pound mushrooms, rinsed and thinly sliced
1 tablespoon minced green onion
1 heaping tablespoon minced fresh Italian parsley
1 heaping tablespoon chopped fresh basil
Salt and freshly ground white pepper to taste

Place the rice in a large pot and rinse it 4 times in cold water. Drain and fill the pot with cold water to a level ¾ inch from the top of the rice. Over high heat bring the rice to a boil and let it boil over medium-high heat until the surface water has been absorbed and the top of the rice is pitted and bubbly (approximately 10 minutes). Cover the pot with a tight-fitting lid and reduce the heat to as low as possible. Simmer covered for another 15 to 20 minutes. Do not let the rice burn. It should be dry and fluffy.

Meanwhile, melt the butter in a skillet and sauté the mushrooms over medium heat for 10 minutes. Add the green onion and sauté 1 minute longer.

Toss the mushrooms, parsley, and basil into the rice, mixing well. Season to taste with salt and pepper and serve.

Oven-roasted Summer Squashes

We used baby squashes in this recipe. If they are unavailable substitute mature squashes, but select the smallest, firmest, and freshest-looking.

10 to 12 baby pattypan squash
10 to 12 baby zucchini
10 to 12 baby crookneck squash
Olive oil
Coarse salt

Preheat the oven to 425°. Wash and dry the squashes.

Rub the squashes with olive oil and sprinkle liberally with coarse salt. Place them on a baking sheet in a single layer and roast for in the preheated oven for 20 minutes, or until they are beginning to brown and are tender when pierced with a skewer.

WHOLE STEAMED FISH WITH DIPPING SAUCES

Chinese Rice Noodles with Bok Choy • Chinese Green Beans with Sesame • Beer

Serves 4

Steaming is one of the healthiest ways to cook fish. It adds no oil or fat, and as most fish are naturally quite low in fat, it keeps the calorie count way down. Steaming also brings out the flavor of the fish and keeps it moist and tender. Steamed fish is a staple in Chinese cuisine, and it is typically served in the center of the table, where each eater helps him or herself to bites with chopsticks. The prized delicacy is the fish cheeks, the small morsel of richly flavored meat just in front of the gills beneath the eyes.

Whole Steamed Fish with Dipping Sauces

Rockfish, black sea bass, ocean perch, porgy, striped bass, grouper, haddock, and catfish are good selections for steaming whole. We get the best results with a covered wok; the fish can be steamed on a steamer, on a plate set on two crossed chopsticks placed in the wok, on top of two parallel chopsticks set in the wok, or on a flat grater positioned in the wok over the steaming liquid. Use whatever method works best for you and your equipment.

>   One 2½ to 3 pound whole dressed fish
>   Salt
>   Chinese Dipping Sauces, page 66
>   1½ cups water
>   ½ cup rice wine or rice wine vinegar
>   Dash of Asian sesame oil
>   2 garlic cloves, chopped
>   1 tablespoon chopped fresh ginger
>   5 thin orange slices

The fish should be scaled and gutted, with the gills removed but the head and tail on. Rinse the fish under running water and pat dry. Sprinkle both sides with salt and allow the fish to sit for 30 minutes at room temperature.

Make 4 deep diagonal slashes in the fish on both sides. Prepare any or all of the dipping sauces and set aside.

Combine the water, rice wine, and sesame oil in a wok. Position the steamer in the wok and place the fish on it. Sprinkle the garlic and ginger over the fish and arrange the orange slices in an overlapping row on top.

Bring the water to a boil, reduce the heat to medium, cover, and steam the fish for 15 to 20 minutes, or 10 minutes per inch of thickness as measured at the thickest part of the fish.

Carefully remove the fish to a serving platter (so it doesn't fall apart) and serve immediately with the dipping sauces.

Chinese Rice Noodles with Bok Choy

>   ¾ pound dried rice noodles
>   1 bunch bok choy
>   1 tablespoon peanut oil
>   Dash of Asian sesame oil
>   2 tablespoons soy sauce
>   2 tablespoons rice vinegar or distilled white vinegar
>   2 tablespoons water
>   ¼ teaspoon salt

Soak the noodles in warm water for 15 minutes. Rinse and drain well in a colander.

Wash, dry, and trim the bottom of the bok choy. Slice diagonally into 3-inch pieces.

In a wok over medium-high heat, heat the peanut and sesame oils. Add the bok choy and stir-fry for 2 minutes. Add the soy sauce, vinegar, water, salt, and drained noodles and stir-fry another 3 minutes. The bok choy should still be slightly crunchy.

Serve immediately.

Chinese Green Beans with Sesame

Prepare this cold bean dish in advance to allow it to marinate.

>   1 tablespoon white sesame seeds
>   ½ pound Chinese long beans or string beans, trimmed
>   and cut into 6-inch pieces
>   1 tablespoon peanut oil
>   1 teaspoon Asian sesame oil
>   1 teaspoon rice vinegar or distilled white vinegar
>   1 tablespoon soy sauce
>   ½ garlic clove, minced to a paste

In a preheated 375° oven, roast the sesame seeds in a single layer until brown, approximately 4 minutes.

Rinse and trim the beans. Steam for 3 to 5 minutes, or until tender but crunchy. Run under cold water to cool. Pat dry and place in a large bowl.

Whisk the oils, vinegar, soy, and garlic together. Toss with the beans and sesame seeds. Marinate 1 hour at room temperature.

BROILED BLUEFISH WITH MUSTARD SEED SAUCE

Sautéed Rosemary Potatoes • Steamed Broccoli • Pumpernickel Rolls
New York Chardonnay

Serves 4

Bluefish is well known to easterners, and many can even claim to have caught their own at one time or another. Anyone who has caught a bluefish is probably also familiar with the peculiar eating habit that earned it the nickname "chopper." Bluefish travel in packs, indulging in eating frenzies that leave little behind. A relatively oily fish, it is best adapted to dry-heat cooking such as broiling or grilling, and it needs no extra fat or oil for cooking.

Broiled Bluefish with Mustard Seed Sauce

Bluefish cooks best with the skin on, especially if you're grilling it. Cook and serve the fish skin side down. The skin is somewhat tough and does not make good eating, but the fish flakes away from the skin quite easily.

Mustard Seed Sauce, page 63
2 bluefish fillets, ¾ pound each

Prepare the Mustard Seed Sauce and set aside in a warm place.

Remove the broiler pan and preheat the broiler. Broil the fish 1½ inches from the heating element for 7 to 8 minutes (for a ¾-inch thick fillet) without turning, or until the flesh near the center has just lost its translucency.

Arrange each serving on a plate and serve with the sauce.

Sautéed Rosemary Potatoes

1 pound small potatoes
¼ cup olive oil
2 teaspoons chopped fresh rosemary,
  or 1 teaspoon dried rosemary
Salt and freshly ground pepper to taste

Scrub the potatoes but do not peel. Slice each one in half. Put them in a large pot, cover with cold water, and bring to a boil. Reduce the heat and simmer covered for 12 minutes. Drain the potatoes and pat dry. Let them cool and slice into bite-sized chunks.

In a large skillet over high heat, heat the oil. Add the potatoes, toss to coat with oil, and sauté until they begin to brown. Add the rosemary and sauté a few minutes more. Drain on paper towels. Season with salt and pepper and serve.

Steamed Broccoli

1½ pounds broccoli
3 tablespoons Crème Fraiche, page 63
Salt and freshly ground white pepper to taste

Wash and trim the broccoli. Cut into uniform-sized pieces. Steam for 10 minutes, or until tender when pierced with a skewer. Do not overcook.

Remove to a serving dish, toss with the Crème Fraiche, and season with salt and pepper.

CIOPPINO

Marinated White Bean Salad with Sliced Tomatoes • Crusty Italian Bread
Beer

Serves 6

According to legend, *cioppino* originated in San Francisco's Italian community. But also according legend, *cioppino* was created by Portuguese fishermen elsewhere in California. Whether Portuguese or Italian in origin, it is a dish that has its roots solidly in California, and it always includes Dungeness crab.

Cioppino

This hearty stew should be served with lots of great bread for soaking up the flavorful sauce.

    2 dozen hard-shell clams
    1 medium-sized Dungeness crab, cooked, cleaned,
        broken into chunks and claws cracked
        (see page 19)
    1½ pounds firm white fish fillets,
        cut into bite-sized pieces and bones removed
    1 pound large raw shrimp, shelled
    ¼ cup olive oil
    2 large onions, chopped
    2 carrots, chopped
    4 garlic cloves, chopped
    1 cup dry red wine
    12 to 15 Italian plum tomatoes, seeded and chopped,
        or 2 large cans Italian plum tomatoes, chopped
    3 cups water
    2 fresh thyme sprigs, chopped,
        or ½ teaspoon dried thyme
    8 large fresh basil leaves, chopped,
        or ½ teaspoon dried basil
    1 teaspoon chopped fresh rosemary,
        or ½ teaspoon dried rosemary
    1½ teaspoons chopped fresh oregano,
        or ½ teaspoon dried oregano
    ¼ teaspoon cayenne
    ¼ teaspoon dried red pepper flakes
    Freshly ground black pepper
    6 parsley sprigs, chopped

Scrub the clams under running water and soak in salted water for half an hour. Allow the rest of the seafood to come to room temperature.

In a large stockpot, heat the olive oil over medium heat and sauté the onions, carrots, and garlic. Add the red wine, increase the heat, and add the clams. Steam the clams in the wine until they open. Remove with a slotted spoon and reserve. Discard any that do not open.

To the wine and clam stock, add the chopped tomatoes, water, thyme, basil, rosemary, oregano, cayenne, pepper flakes, and several grindings of black pepper. Simmer 30 to 45 minutes.

Add the cooked crab pieces and simmer 2 minutes. Add the fish chunks and shrimp and cook 5 minutes more, or until the shrimp and fish are opaque. Add the clams and reheat for another minute or so.

Ladle the stew into large heated bowls and serve with chopped parsley on top.

Marinated White Bean Salad with Sliced Tomatoes

    1 cup dried Great Northern or small white beans
    2 cups chicken broth
    4 cups water
    Bay leaf
    1-inch piece of dried red pepper
    ½ teaspoon salt
    ¼ cup virgin olive oil
    ½ tablespoon red wine vinegar
    2 garlic cloves, minced to a paste
        with a pinch of salt
    6 large fresh basil leaves, chopped,
        or ½ teaspoon dried basil
    2 tablespoons chopped fresh parsley
    ½ small red onion, sliced paper thin
    Freshly ground black pepper
    3 ripe beefsteak tomatoes, sliced

Rinse the beans in a colander and pick out any rocks. Soak the beans overnight in 3 times as much water.

Drain the beans and put them in a large stockpot with the chicken broth, water, bay leaf, red pepper, and salt. Cook covered over low heat until the beans are tender but not mushy, approximately 1 hour.

Drain off all the liquid and remove the bay leaf and pepper. Combine the olive oil, vinegar, garlic, basil, and parsley in a small bowl. Pour over the hot beans, add the onion, and toss well to combine. Season to taste with black pepper. Allow the beans to cool to room temperature before serving, and serve over sliced fresh tomatoes.

YELLOWTAIL, TUNA, AND HALIBUT SASHIMI

Steamed Rice with Nori Strips • Cucumber Salad • Sake

Serves 4

This light but protein-rich *sashimi* menu is perfect for lunch. Select the *freshest* fish for *sashimi* from only the most reputable fish markets. The best place to buy are Japanese markets where the fishmonger is accustomed to selling fish for *sashimi* and *sushi*. Tell the fishmonger that you will be eating the fish raw and ask for his or her advice. Other types of fish may be more suitable or in season at the time you are buying, but the key requirement is the utmost freshness.

Yellowtail, Tuna, and Halibut Sashimi

Sashimi Dipping Sauce, page 66
¼ pound yellowtail fillet
¼ pound tuna fillet
¼ pound halibut fillet

Prepare the Sashimi Dipping Sauce and set aside.

Skin the fillets. Remove the dark muscle from the tuna if this has not already been done.

Trim the fillets into uniform rectangles. With each fillet flat on a board, slice thin, even slices with the grain of the fish.

Arrange the sliced fish on a serving platter and serve with Sashimi Dipping Sauce.

Steamed Rice with Nori Strips

Nori is the Japanese name for seaweed. It tastes slightly toasted and slightly salty, and its nutritive value is sky-high. Seaweed is among the most nutritionally perfect foods in the world. You can find dried sheets of it in Japanese markets or natural foods stores. Our rice is a vinegar-flavored rice similar to that used in *sushi*.

2 cups unconverted short-grained rice
½ teaspoon salt
3 tablespoons rice vinegar or distilled white vinegar
Scant 1 tablespoon sugar
1 *nori* sheet, sliced into ¼-inch by 2-inch strips

Put the rice in a large pot. Wash and drain it in 4 changes of water. Put enough water in the pot to come up to a level ½ inch above the top of the rice. Add the salt to the water.

Over high heat, bring the rice to a boil. Stir once, cover tightly, reduce the heat, and simmer the rice for 20 minutes. Turn off the heat and allow the rice to stand, covered and undisturbed, for another 15 minutes.

Meanwhile, heat the rice vinegar and sugar in a small stainless steel saucepan.

Put the rice into a large serving bowl. Add the sweetened rice vinegar to the rice a little at a time, tossing to coat and cool the rice. Fan the rice with a folded sheet of paper while tossing to bring out a shiny coating. Mix in the *nori* strips with a fork one at a time to keep them from sticking to each other.

Cucumber Salad

1 cucumber, sliced into ⅛-inch rounds
½ cup cider vinegar
1 tablespoon sugar
1 teaspoon white sesame seeds

Slice the cucumber rounds in half.

In a small stainless steel saucepan, combine the vinegar and sugar and heat until the sugar is dissolved. Remove from heat and allow to cool.

Pour the cooled sweetened vinegar over the cucumber slices and marinate for half an hour at room temperature. Sprinkle the sesame seeds on top and serve.

OYSTERS ON THE HALF SHELL

Fish Mousse with Lemon Butter Sauce and Flying Fish Roe • Cold New Asparagus
with Red Pepper Mayonnaise • Bread Sticks • Dry White Wine

Serves 6

This informal meal makes an elegant springtime lunch. The mousse can be prepared in advance and brought to room temperature before serving, and the asparagus is served cold, so nothing is left to do but open the oysters and pop them into your mouth (that is if your guests will allow you to take one for yourself!). The oysters may be opened in advance, but in a casual setting you can open them on demand.

Oysters on the Half Shell

We call for 40 oysters, which is 6 per person plus a few extras in case some just won't open. We like our oysters without any sauce save maybe a few drops of lemon juice, so the Seafood Sauce is optional for those who prefer it. See page 24 for information on oysters.

40 fresh oysters
Lemon wedges
Seafood Sauce, page 65 (optional)

Select oysters that are tightly closed and feel slightly heavy. Very lightweight ones should be avoided. Store oysters cup side down in the refrigerator for no more than 2 days.

Scrub the shells with a brush under cold running water.

To shuck: Hold the oysters cup side down with a mitt or towel between you and the oyster. (You will want to hold the oyster as steadily as possible so as not to lose much of the liquor inside.) Using an oyster knife, work the tip of the knife between the shells very near the hinge. Slide the knife around sidewise and twist and pry upward until you hear the shell crack open. Run the tip of the knife all around the inside edges of the shell, prying upward to loosen further. Slide the knife along the top of the shell to sever the muscle from the top. Do not puncture the oyster. Pull off the top shell. Sever the oyster from the bottom of the shell and serve immediately with lemon wedges, and seafood sauce if desired.

Fish Mousse with Lemon Butter Sauce and Flying Fish Roe

Seafood mousses can be made from many types of fish. Do not use frozen fish, as it adds moisture that throws off the delicate balance in mousse-making. A well-chilled firm white-fleshed fish such as snapper, angler, sea bass, or cod is best. Try also shellfish such as scallops, shrimp, or lobster. All fish should be skinless, and as boneless as possible. Chilling all the ingredients (and even the utensils, if you have the time) is important. If you use a blender, prepare the recipe in two batches. Capers are a delicious substitution for the roe if desired.

1 pound chilled firm white fish
Softened butter
2 eggs
2 shallots, minced
1 heaping tablespoon chopped fresh tarragon,
**   or a pinch of dried tarragon**
Pinch of cayenne
Pinch of ground nutmeg
½ teaspoon salt
¼ teaspoon freshly ground white pepper
1½ cups cold heavy cream
Lemon Butter Sauce, page 62
1 heaping tablespoon flying fish roe

Make sure you are starting out with *cold* fish, as this is essential to making a successful mousse. Cube the fish, checking carefully for bones. Place the fish in the bowl of a food processor with the blade inserted, and refrigerate until ready to use.

Preheat the oven to 350° and put a teakettle of water on to boil. Keep the water hot. Butter a 4 to 6 cup mold with softened butter and place in the refrigerator.

Remove the food processor bowl with the fish from the refrigerator. Process for a few seconds. Add the eggs, shallots, tarragon, cayenne, nutmeg, salt and pepper and process for 1 minute. Add the cream with the motor running and process until smooth, another minute or so.

Press the mixture into the chilled mold and smooth the top. Cover tightly with buttered aluminum foil cut to size.

Place the mold in a baking dish with high sides. Fill the baking dish with enough hot water to come halfway up the sides of the mold. Bake in the preheated oven for approximately 40 minutes.

Just before the mousse has finished cooking, prepare the Lemon Butter Sauce and keep warm over gentle heat.

Allow the mousse to cool for 10 minutes. Carefully invert onto a serving platter. Serve at room temperature with sauce and sprinkle with roe.

Cold New Asparagus with Red Pepper Mayonnaise

2 pounds thin asparagus
Red Pepper Mayonnaise, page 59

Rinse the asparagus and bend each stalk carefully until it breaks at its natural breaking point (this removes the stringy end). Steam for 5 minutes or until just tender and bright green but still crunchy. Cool immediately under cold running water.

Drain the spears and pat dry. Keep in the refrigerator or at room temperature until ready to serve.

Prepare the mayonnaise.

Arrange the spears on a platter and give each diner an individual serving of mayonnaise for dipping.

CRAB ENCHILADAS WITH SALSA VERDE

Scallop Seviche • Tortilla Chips and Guacamole
Colorful Shredded Salad

Serves 4 to 6

Many delicious seafood recipes come to us from Latin America, where, particularly along the coasts, diverse cuisines abound in fish and shellfish dishes. One of the most popular is a dish of Peruvian origin called *seviche,* fish marinated in lime juice until "cooked." This type of marinade is one of the simplest forms of pickling, and though it does not have the shelf life of a true pickle, it can preserve fish for up to a week. The citric acid in the lime reacts with the proteins in the fish, turning it firm and opaque just as if it were cooked with heat.

Crab Enchiladas with Salsa Verde

Salsa Verde, page 68
2 tablespoons peanut oil
12 corn tortillas
3 cups fresh lump crab meat (about 1¼ pounds)
1 cup sour cream
½ red onion, minced
Salt and freshly ground white pepper
½ cup grated jack cheese or other mild cheese
2 green onions, white part only, sliced

Prepare the Salsa Verde and set aside.

Preheat the oven to 375°.

Heat the peanut oil in a cast iron pan or heavy skillet over medium-high heat. Quickly heat the tortillas in the oil, allowing just a few seconds per side. They will puff up for a moment. Remove to drain on paper towels.

Mix the crab meat with ½ cup of the sour cream, ½ cup of the *salsa verde,* and minced onion. Blend well. Season to taste with salt and pepper and set aside.

Spread a thin layer of *salsa verde* in the bottom of a casserole large enough to hold 12 rolled enchiladas. Place 1 tortilla flat on a board and put 2 heaping tablespoons of crab filling down the middle. Roll the tortilla around the filling and place seam side down in the casserole. Continue with the rest of the tortillas.

Spread the remaining *salsa verde* over the enchiladas. Mix the grated cheese with the remaining ½ cup of sour cream and put a dollop on each enchilada. Sprinkle chopped green onion over the top. Bake in the preheated oven for 25 minutes, or until piping hot. Serve immediately.

Scallop Seviche

Any firm white-fleshed fish or shellfish can be used in seviche.

1 pound scallops
Seviche Marinade, page 65
1 small tomato, seeded and chopped
Salt and freshly ground black pepper
3 cilantro sprigs, chopped

If you are using large sea scallops, slice them with a sharp knife into bite-sized pieces.

Prepare the seviche marinade. Combine with the scallops in a glass or earthenware bowl.

Cover with a clean kitchen cloth and set in a cool place to marinate. Marinate the fish for 2 to 3 hours (or 4 to 6 hours in the refrigerator), tossing from time to time. Just before serving, add the chopped tomato and season to taste with salt and pepper. Sprinkle freshly chopped cilantro on top of each serving. You can serve the *seviche* with the marinade liquid, or spoon each serving out with a slotted spoon to drain off the liquid.

Tortilla Chips and Guacamole

Look for fresh yellow or blue corn tortillas in the specialty section of your grocery. Cut them into triangles and fry in hot peanut oil for fresh chips. Or if time is short, buy good-quality tortilla chips. Select avocados that are very ripe—soft at the top end but not mushy. Underripe avocados just don't make good *guacamole.*

Japapeño chilies will make a spicy *guacamole.* For an even spicier (hotter) *guacamole,* do not seed the *jalapeño.*

2 large ripe avocados
¼ red onion, minced
½ tomato, seeded and chopped
½ fresh mild green chili such as *poblano* or Anaheim, minced
½ *jalapeño* chili, seeded and minced, optional
Juice of 1 lime or ¼ lemon
1 small garlic clove, minced
8 cilantro sprigs, chopped
Salt and freshly ground black pepper

Peel and seed the avocados. Place in a large bowl and mash well with a fork or potato masher. Mix in the remaining ingredients and season with salt and pepper to taste.

Colorful Shredded Salad

½ head red leaf lettuce
½ head romaine or green leaf lettuce
1 Belgian endive
5 tablespoons olive oil
1 tablespoon red wine vinegar
1 teaspoon Dijon mustard
Small pinch of sugar
Salt and freshly ground black pepper to taste
½ red onion, thinly sliced
⅓ cup crumbled blue cheese

Wash and dry the lettuces and Belgian endive. Slice the red leaf lettuce and romaine horizontally into ¼-inch strips. Slice the endive vertically into ¼-inch strips.

Combine the olive oil, vinegar, mustard, and sugar in the bottom of a salad bowl. Season with salt and pepper. Pile the lettuces, endive, onion, and crumbled blue cheese on top and toss just before serving.

BROILED SWORDFISH STEAKS WITH TARTAR SAUCE

White and Wild Rice with Green Onion • Julienned Zucchini and Carrots
Arugula and Butter Lettuce with Walnut Dressing • Dry White Wine

Serves 4

Swordfish, so-named for the obvious weapon it wears on its snout, is capable of impaling small vessels and large fish. But the delicious, almost beeflike flavor of this fearless fish has earned it a great deal of popularity. Swordfish eating was once limited to sportfishermen and a very limited commercial market because of the difficulty in catching it. But with modernized fishing methods, the swordfish is widely available and increasingly appreciated. It is particularly delicious broiled or grilled, but do not overcook it as it tends to get dry very quickly.

Broiled Swordfish Steaks with Tartar Sauce

For best results when broiling fish, put the fish on a cold broiler pan rather than preheating the broiler with the pan in it. Placing fish on a hot broiler pan begins to cook the underside, and overcooks the other side once you turn it.

> Tartar Sauce, page 59
> 2 tablespoons olive oil
> 2 tablespoons butter
> 2 teaspoons Dijon mustard
> 1 teaspoon white wine vinegar
> Freshly ground pepper to taste
> 4 swordfish steaks, ⅓ pound each

Prepare the Tartar Sauce and set aside.

Remove the broiler pan and preheat the broiler.

In a small saucepan over low heat, combine the olive oil, butter, mustard, vinegar, and pepper and whisk until melted and smooth. Place the steaks on the cold broiler pan and brush the tops with the oil and mustard basting sauce.

Broil the steaks approximately 3 inches from the heating element for 6 minutes. Turn the steaks, baste the other side, and broil another 5 minutes. The center should still be just a little bit pink.

Serve with Tartar Sauce.

White and Wild Rice with Green Onion

The hearty flavor of wild rice is excellent with swordfish.

> ½ cup wild rice
> 2 cups chicken broth
> 1 cup water
> 1 cup unconverted long-grain white rice
> 1 green onion, including half the green leaves,
>   chopped
> 2 tablespoons butter
> 3 tablespoons chopped fresh parsley
> Salt and freshly ground black pepper to taste

Wash the wild rice thoroughly under running water. Place in a large pot with the chicken broth and water and bring to a boil. Boil uncovered over medium heat for 10 minutes.

While the wild rice is boiling, rinse the white rice under running water until the water runs clear. When the wild rice has boiled for 10 minutes, add the white rice and green onion and cook another 10 minutes uncovered.

Reduce the heat and cover the pot with a tight-fitting lid. Cook over very low heat 10 to 15 minutes longer, or until both types of rice are tender and all the liquid is gone.

Toss the cooked rice with the butter and parsley. Season to taste and serve.

Julienned Zucchini and Carrots

> 3 medium-sized zucchini
> 4 carrots
> 2 tablespoons butter
> Salt and freshly ground pepper

Wash and trim the zucchini and carrots; peel the carrots. With a very sharp knife or a food processor fitted with the julienne blade, cut the zucchini and carrots into long ⅛-inch julienne strips.

Steam for 3 to 5 minutes, or until tender but still crunchy. Toss with the butter, season to taste, and serve immediately.

Arugula and Butter Lettuce with Walnut Dressing

> 1 bunch *arugula*
> 1 head butter lettuce
> ¼ cup walnuts
>
> *Dressing:*
> 4½ tablespoons walnut oil
> 1 tablespoon white wine vinegar
> 1 tablespoon chopped fresh parsley
> Pinch of sugar
> Salt and freshly ground black pepper to taste

Wash and dry the arugula and lettuce leaves. Toast the walnuts in a preheated 375° oven for 5 to 7 minutes, or until they are just beginning to darken slightly. Set aside to cool.

Combine the oil, vinegar, parsley, sugar, and salt and pepper and whisk until emulsified.

Break the lettuce leaves into pieces and toss with the dressing. Sprinkle each serving with broken toasted walnuts.

SOUP SAMPLER

Lobster Bisque • Oyster Stew • Manhattan Clam Chowder
Bread Board • Champagne

Serves 10 to 12

We call this menu our "Soup Sampler:" three different soups to serve for a late-night supper. Or you can serve any one these soups with a simple salad, bread, and wine as a delicious meal for six people.

Lobster Bisque

Serves 6

Lobster bisque is an elegant soup with a beautiful color and delicate flavor. One of our favorites.

> **3 cups White Wine Fish Stock, page 58**
> **One 1½ pound live female lobster,**
>   **killed and cleaned (see page 23),**
>   **coral and tomalley reserved**
> **6 tablespoons butter**
> **1 carrot, chopped**
> **1 small onion, chopped**
> **1 celery stalk, chopped**
> **½ cup cognac**
> **1 cup dry white wine**
> **2 cups water**
> **1 tablespoon tomato paste**
> **1 garlic clove, slightly crushed**
> **Bay leaf**
> **2 fresh thyme sprigs,**
>   **or 1 large pinch dried thyme**
> **4 parsley sprigs**
> **6 white peppercorns**
> **3 tablespoons flour**
> **Coral and tomalley of the lobster**
> **1 cup heavy cream**
> **Salt and freshly ground white pepper to taste**
> **Fresh chives**

Prepare the fish stock and set aside.

Crack the lobster claws and cut the body and tail into several large chunks.

In a deep sauté pan or large skillet, melt 3 tablespoons of the butter. Cook the carrot, onion, and celery in the butter until soft, about 5 minutes.

Add the lobster chunks and sauté over high heat for 2 to 3 minutes. Reduce the heat, add the cognac to the pan, allow it to simmer for 10 seconds, and carefully ignite it. When the flames die down, cover the pan and simmer until the lobster shells turn bright red. Remove the lobster and set aside.

To the pan add the wine, fish stock, water, tomato paste, garlic clove, bay leaf, thyme, parsley sprigs, and peppercorns and begin simmering uncovered over low heat. Meanwhile, pick all the cooked lobster meat from the shells and set aside.

Break the shells into small pieces by hand or with a mallet or cleaver. Add the shells to the pan, cover, and simmer for 1 hour.

Strain the broth through a fine sieve, pressing down on the vegetables and shells to remove all the liquid. Discard the solids. Strain the broth again through several layers of cheesecloth back into the pan.

In a small saucepan, melt the remaining 3 tablespoons of butter over medium-low heat and add the flour, whisking constantly. Cook the flour for 3 minutes. Add 1 cup of the broth and whisk until smooth. Whisk this back into the broth in the pan. Cook and stir over low heat for 5 minutes, or until thick and smooth. Whisk the coral and tomalley into the cream until well blended and add this to the broth. Slice the lobster meat into thin bite-sized pieces and add to the soup. Adjust the seasoning and heat through. Do not allow the soup to come to a boil.

Garnish with fresh minced chives and 2 or 3 chive spears.

Oyster Stew

Serves 4

You can use the shucked oysters packed in jars, but fresh ones will make a difference. Blue Points are the best suited for stew, but try any small oyster. See page 24 for information on cleaning and shucking oysters.

> **16 fresh small to medium-sized oysters**
> **6 tablespoons butter**
> **2 tablespoon dry sherry**
> **2 dashes celery salt**
> **Dash of Worcestershire sauce**
> **3 cups half and half**
> **Fresh thyme sprig**
> **Salt and freshly ground white pepper to taste**
> **1 tablespoon minced fresh parsley**
> **Paprika**

Shuck the oysters over a bowl to catch all the liquor. Strain the liquor through several layers of cheesecloth or squeeze through a coffee filter and reserve.

In the top of a double boiler over barely simmering water (the water should not touch the bottom of the top pan), melt 4 tablespoons of the butter with the sherry, celery salt, and Worcestershire sauce.

Add the oysters, checking each one for tiny shell shards. Stir the oysters very gently in the butter, and cook just until the edges are beginning to curl, approximately 1 minute. Add the reserved oyster liquor, half and half, and thyme sprig and heat through, stirring frequently. Do not boil. Remove the thyme sprig and season with salt and pepper. Ladle into soup bowls. Put ½ tablespoon butter on each serving, and sprinkle with parsley and paprika.

Recipe for Manhattan Clam
Chowder on following page.

Manhattan Clam Chowder

Serves 4 to 6

Cherrystones or littlenecks are best for this chowder, but
try also chowder clams or even the giant geoduck. Cooking
the broth with the empty clam shells enhances the flavor
of the chowder.

> **48 hard-shell clams, scrubbed and soaked**
>   **(see page 17)**
> **2 heaping tablespoons diced salt pork**
> **1 onion, chopped**
> **1 celery stalk, chopped**
> **1 small green bell pepper, seeded and chopped**
> **1 potato, diced**
> **4 large tomatoes, seeded and pureed**
> **1 fresh thyme sprig, or a large pinch of dried thyme**
> **Bay leaf**
> **Dash of cayenne**
> **Salt and freshly ground black pepper**
> **Chopped fresh parsley**

Shuck all but 6 clams over a bowl to catch the juice. Set
the 6 unshucked clams and 6 empty clam shells aside. Strain
the juice through several layers of cheesecloth or squeeze
through a coffee filter. Add water as necessary to make 1½
cups and set aside. Chop the clams coarsely.

In a large pot, render the salt pork over low heat until crispy.
Add the onion, celery, and green pepper and sauté over
medium heat until translucent, approximately 10 minutes.
Add the diced potatoes and sauté 3 more minutes.

Add the reserved clam juice, the 6 empty clam shells, pureed
tomatoes, thyme, bay leaf, and cayenne and simmer gently
until the potatoes are nearly done, approximately 20 minutes.
Remove the empty shells, thyme sprig, and bay leaf and
discard.

Add the 6 whole clams and the chopped clams and cook
5 to 7 minutes, until the chopped clams are just firm and
opaque but still tender, and the whole clams are open. Do
not overcook.

Season to taste with salt and pepper. Ladle each serving
into a soup bowl and place the open clam on top. Sprinkle
with parsley and serve.

BIBLIOGRAPHY

Anderson, Ken. *The Gourmet's Guide to Fish and Shellfish*. New York: Quill, 1984.

Cronin, Isaac, Harlow, Jay, and Johnson, Paul. *The California Seafood Cookbook*. Berkeley, CA: Aris Books, 1983.

Hodgson, Moira. *The New York Times Gourmet Shopper*. New York: Times Books, 1983.

King, Shirley. *Saucing the Fish.*.New York: Simon & Schuster, 1986.

McClane, A. J. *The Encyclopedia of Fish Cookery*. New York: Holt, Rinehart and Winston, 1977.

Morris, Dan, and Morris, Inez. *The Complete Fish Cookbook*. New York: MacMillan Publishing Company, 1972, 1986.

Spinazzola, Anthony, and Paimblanc, Jean-Jacques. *Seafood As We Like It*. Chester, CT: The Globe Pequot Press, 1985.

Tannahill, Reay. *Food in History*. New York: Stein and Day, 1973.